MW00698787

THE MAGNA ILLUSTRATED GUIDE TO
PIGEONS
OF THE WORLD

THE MAGNA ILLUSTRATED GUIDE TO
PIGEONS
OF THE WORLD

Andrew McNeillie

Illustrations by Johan Lentink,
with additional illustrations by
Stephen Cocking and Graham Smith

MAGNA BOOKS

First published in Great Britain by Elsevier Phaidon
(an imprint of Phaidon Press Limited)

© 1976 Andromeda Oxford Ltd

This edition published in 1993 by Magna Books
Magna Road
Leicester LE18 4ZH

ISBN 1 85422 441 7

Printed in Singapore

PREFACE

PIGEONS HAVE been kept for thousands of years and in that time innumerable breeds and varieties have been developed. This guide describes all the major extant breeds of domestic pigeon and records their histories as far as can be done with accuracy. It will be of value both to the expert pigeon fancier and to the beginner, for whom the introductory chapters on pigeon keeping are specifically designed.

In order to help the reader gain an overall picture of the general lines pursued by fanciers over the centuries, the guide section, which forms the main part of the book, has been divided into four sections, each dealing with a particular group of breeds. The descriptions are arranged so that they face the appropriate illustrations, of which there is at least one for every breed discussed. In his research into the historical development of each breed the author has been sobered by the words of Charles Darwin in his *Origin of Species* to the effect that "a breed, like a dialect of a language, can hardly be said to have a distinct origin." Nevertheless, the reader will find this one of the most detailed and comprehensive studies of pigeon breeds that has been published.

Acknowledgements

This book owes its existence in great measure to the efforts of Mr Johan Lentink, whose expert advice, diligence and patience have proved invaluable, and to the researches of Mr Lexi Hiscocks, whom I thank particularly for his corrections and suggested improvements, and for his material on ailments and on showing. Mr Hugh Foster and Mr Wally Foster are also to be thanked. Their part in this book is immeasurable.

A.M.

Note

Two types of cross-reference are used in the breed descriptions. Where the reader is directed from one breed or variety to another in the same section the form "the Gazzi Modena (above)" is used. Where the reference is to a breed or variety in another section the section in which it appears is given in the form "the Leghorn Runt (Section A)."

CONTENTS

LIST OF BREEDS ILLUSTRATED

8

FEATHER AND DISPLAY PIGEONS

COLOR AND TOY PIGEONS

List of breeds illustrated continued

11

List of breeds illustrated continued

Polish Highflier *page 153*
White-saddled Belgian Highflier *page 153*
Danzig Highflier *page 153*

INTRODUCTION

IT IS IMPOSSIBLE to ascertain but it would seem likely that man first kept pigeons as a source of food. The Egyptians had been doing so for some time by c2500 BC – indeed they are still noted for their dove houses and table pigeons. Earlier evidence, from Mesopotamia, in the form of sacred pigeon images dedicated to Astarte, goddess of love and fertility, and dating back to c3000 BC, proves however that there was another side to man's interest in the pigeon. It is this that we see represented in classical and biblical myth. The ancient Greeks held the pigeon to be sacred to Aphrodite and the Romans associated it with Venus, though both also kept pigeons for the table. In the Bible, the dove shares a place with the lamb as a creature of sacrifice. It was the dove, this time in its other important role, as a message bearer, that returned to Noah bearing an olive leaf as evidence of the Flood's subsidence. To Christians the dove became the symbol of the Holy Spirit and among Moslems it has always been held in reverence. In cultures where white is the color of death a white pigeon has sometimes been carried in funeral processions and in the US white stuffed pigeons have been used as a symbol of purity and peace as decorations upon floral tributes at burials.

The pigeon is written into our culture and we still see it in symbolic terms, as a bird of peace and freedom. All of which tends to lend irony to one other use man has found for the pigeon: the role of wartime message bearer. The pigeon was a faster means of communication than either rider or runner and it is said to have been used by the early Persians, Assyrians, Egyptians and Phoenicians to carry military intelligence but the evidence is scant until about 500 BC. The Romans certainly kept pigeons for this purpose over 2000 years ago – contemporary reports describe Julius Caesar making use of them during his conquest of Gaul – and the practice persisted through later centuries. There is ample evidence to prove, for example, that pigeons were used as message carriers by the Saracen armies at the time of the Crusades, and that the crusaders brought pigeons back with them to Europe. They were used during the siege of Acre, and at the sieges of Mansourah and Jerusalem. In Europe they carried news from the outside world to the people of besieged Leyden in the Netherlands and were used by the Venetians during the siege of Venice.

It was the sensational use of pigeons during the Siege of Paris (1871) that gave impetus to the, by then, emergent sport of pigeon racing. The citizens of

the French capital, surrounded by the Prussian army, used hot air balloons to carry men and messages above and beyond the enemy lines and with them went Parisian pigeons. From places as distant as London and Tours these birds then carried communications back to the beleaguered French. At first paper messages were rolled tight, waxed and attached to a tail feather of the bird but many of these were lost. Later they were inserted into a hollow goose quill and tied to the bird with strong silk thread. To enable each bird to carry more communications the French employed the microdot technique which

On the Greek island of Mykonos dovecotes with intricately patterned openings for the birds form a special feature of the island buildings.

Left: a basket of pigeons is loaded onto a balloon during the Siege of Paris. *(Mansell Collection)*

appears so frequently in tales of modern spies: each message was photographed, the image reduced in size, and printed upon a thin film of collodion. Each piece of film could carry about 2,500 communications and up to 12 of these films could be carried by a single bird. At the receiving end the image was projected upon a screen to be read and transcribed if necessary. During four months of the siege no less than 1,150,000 different communications were carried into Paris in this way. The Prussian forces, aware of the use the French were making of their pigeons used trained hawks to intercept them.

An unusual Scottish dovecote with a "shoe shaped" roof at Phantassie, East Lothian, which still houses a few pigeons.

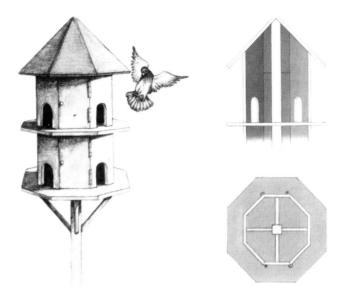

A garden dovecot mounted on a pole should be designed so that cats cannot climb up to or leap on to the landing platform.

In the years that followed, German, Russian, Italian and French governments all set up military pigeon lofts and, despite the advance of electronic communications they were used by armies in both World Wars. They became a standard equipment for a wide range of fighting units, notably those operating deep within the enemy lines. Pigeons could often get through when all else failed. A measure of their importance can be seen from the German action, when they entered Belgium or French territory in World War I, of ordering all pigeons to be destroyed.

Britain and the US were slow to realize the advantages the pigeon had but they too established pigeon corps and played their part in carrying messages from airplanes "ditched" at sea and from minesweepers as well as at the front. Pigeons were trained to fly at night and to home to mobile "combat lofts". They saved many lives and produced their own war heroes, most famous was Cher Ami, an English bred bird serving with a battalion from New York on the Verdun front during World War I. Despite having a leg shattered and his head wounded almost as soon as he was released he flew the 40 kilometres to his base loft in 25 minutes, his message carrier attached to the wounded leg which dangled on a few shreds of sinew. In World War II the Dickin Medal, established in 1943, was awarded to 32 pigeons in recognition of outstanding services. The pigeon played a vital role in carrying messages from American agents dropped behind the lines during the Korean war, but in 1956 the US Army sold the last of its birds and now relies upon electronic devices.

In the more routine role of postal messengers pigeons also have an interesting history. They appear to have been in some way associated with the Greek Oracles and were used by Egyptian ships to give notice of their arrival in port. The Sultan of Baghdad established a pigeon postal system in the 12th century. They were used to carry news of sporting events by both the Greeks and Romans. Their more recent history is outlined elsewhere in this Guide (see Section D, under the entry Homer). Today's Carrier Pigeon (Section A, Carrier) is not of the type one would use as a messenger, and it is not clear whether its true progenitors were ever used for the purpose. But several early treatises do refer to the use of so-called Carriers to carry messages. In one, written in 1765, we can read of a pigeon, "called a Carrier because it is frequently made use of to carry a letter from one place to another; and such is the sagacity of the bird, that though you carry them hood-winked 20 or 30 miles, nay, I have known them to be carried three score or 100, and then turned loose, they will immediately hasten to the place where they were bred. The Dutch call this pigeon Bagadat, probably from a corruption of the name of the city Bagdat (*sic*) from when it came." Modern telecommunications have all but totally ousted the pigeon as post-man. I say "all but" advisedly. In March 1976, in the first elections held in Cuba since Fidel Castro and the communists came to power, pigeons were reported to have been used to carry results from certain outlying areas.

Between the poles of reverence for the pigeon and hard-headedness concerning its utility, is a world that is perhaps best described as one of fond though entirely earnest curiosity. This is the world of the pigeon fancier and the true province of this book. It cannot be treated in isolation from the functional, for it both contributes to and benefits from it. The cultivation of table or squabbing pigeons for commercial purposes, for example, has greatly strengthened the fancy in America, and vice versa. But the great diversity of breeds and varieties owes its existence to purist interest more than to any other single factor. In order to appreciate the range of achievement it is useful to have before us the specifications of what might be called the basic ingredient in all this, namely the Rock Dove *Columba livia*. This bird is native to Europe, India and western Asia, and North Africa. It is bluish-gray in color with black wing bars, white loins and a bar at the end of the tail. The Rock Dove haunts rocky uplands and coastal cliffs, roosting and nesting in caves and on rock-ledges. Since Charles Darwin made his study of the domestic pigeon, in the mid-19th century, it has been generally accepted that the Rock Dove is the common ancestor of all our fancy pigeons. A substantial part of the evidence Darwin offers in support of his theory hinges on the pronounced tendency for basic Rock Dove coloring to reappear at one stage or another in all domestic breeds. He points out that although the domestic pigeons differ widely from each other and from the Rock Dove, the main differences are more external than structural. As may be seen from a comparison of, say, the Carrier (Section A), the Fantail (Section B) the Oriental Frills (Section C) and the Rock Dove, this claim is not always easy to believe.

A Greek gravestone of 500 BC.

THE CARE OF PIGEONS

Housing

The principles involved in housing pigeons correctly are the same whether you have an acre of ground and money in your pocket or only the corner of a backyard and the proceeds of a newspaper round to build upon. If your resources are slender and you find that all you can run to is a pair or two of birds, you should not by any means be discouraged. A modest start is not simply better than none, it is possibly best of all, for there is much to learn and lessons are generally easiest where they are plain and simple.

This chapter outlines two basic structures upon which the fancier-to-be might improvise, according to his circumstances and particular interests.

A simple box-house

Should you plan to make your start with just a pair of racing or highflying pigeons, then you will need no more than a pretty simple box-like structure. Pigeons are best managed where they have neither too little nor too much living room. The exact proportions you build to may vary slightly but, in the case of a home for two performing birds, a structure with a floor plan $3' \times 2'6''$ and a height at the rear of $2'6''$ dropping by up to $6''$ to the front is ideal. It may be free-standing or else leaning-to against a wall, which is possibly the most convenient form, provided there are no drainage problems to create damp. Either way the box must be weather-proof, ideally facing away from the prevailing wind, or if this is not entirely possible, suitably shielded either by surrounding buildings or a screen of fencing. If there is room for choice, a southerly aspect is to be preferred. The roof needs to be felted and well lipped, and, in the case of lean-to houses, should slant to the front.

Care must be taken to eliminate draughts while at the same time maintaining good ventilation. These points are vital to the health of your birds, which must be kept in a dry, airy environment in order to thrive well. Draughts can be stopped by structural adjustments and strategically placed vents can help regulate the air-flow, but these alone cannot keep the atmosphere in a pigeon house good and fresh. The birds must also be kept clean and their droppings scraped up and cleared away as regularly as possible. Bear this in mind when constructing your house and be sure to allow yourself easy access to corners where dirt might accumulate and foster disease. In this respect the

A small box-house, suitable for keeping a pair of pigeons. It can be either free-standing or built against a wall. Additional weatherboarding can be hinged on the side and kept open by a hook on to one of the legs, with hooks at the top to keep it in a closed position. The whole box should be sited so that the prevailing wind does not blow into it. The exact proportions of such a house will vary according to the space available but those given here are suitable for a pair of performing birds. Fancy breeds should also have a wired-in flight area of at least 6 ft in length.

design of the front of the box is most important. Ideally it should consist of a single section hinged to the floor and so opening fully to facilitate cleaning. One half of the front should be board, the other should be wired with half-inch mesh or, preferably, barred vertically with dowel, and should contain an entrance, about 6" in width. As shown in the diagram, the entrance door can be constructed so as to provide an interior perch when closed and an exterior landing area when open. Catches for attaching additional weather-boards should also be fitted. Inside you will need to fit two perches (the inverted-V type is ideal) at either end, and a further perching board along the back, about mid-way up. The box itself should be placed at a convenient height so that you can tend the birds without stooping. You should be able to feed by hand, thus strengthening your relationship with the birds, and, to avoid cluttering up the floor area, a drinker may be attached outside, the birds' access being through the open-work front.

Pairs of cocks or hens soon adapt and can be kept with great success under these conditions, but you will learn more of the art of pigeon fancying, and probably gain greater satisfaction, by keeping a true pair, although in this case you must be careful not to allow your birds' natural enthusiasm for each other to get the better of your pocket. Young birds present a considerable problem when one is operating on such a small scale. But if it is not always feasible to breed for sale, there is always the table to be considered. One way or another, if you are going to breed, then you will need a second box in which to wean the young. This of course can be less elaborate in design, though it must conform to most of the general requirements outlined above. If your interests run to one of the fancy breeds, you would be well advised to extend the basic box by providing a wired-in flight area. At least a 6ft flight is required, so if you do not have the room it is perhaps wisest to steer clear of the majority of fancy breeds.

The basic loft
Anything from converted railway carriage to garden shed will serve as a pigeon loft, but a specially designed loft is plainly going to be easier to work with. The ideal to be discussed here is a structure of $18' \times 6'$, in three $6' \times 6'$ units, with a maximum height from floor to ceiling of 7'. With a set-up of this kind there is room to accommodate old birds, to hive off young birds as the breeding season progresses, and to segregate the sexes during the off-season. In terms of numbers kept, it is perhaps best to think of the large three-part loft as if it consisted of two units only – the third being a reserve area. On this basis, you have room for a stock of 15–18 pairs. The ratio of pigeons to loft-space is important. Overhousing, that is, providing too much room, creates wild and unmanageable birds and is as undesirable as its opposite, which creates unhealthy conditions. Both can of course be remedied: the former by partitioning, the latter by culling; but it is as well to calculate how many birds one can afford to keep through the year, to build accordingly, and to abide pretty strictly by that ratio.

A wooden-floored loft must be raised on brick or concrete piers, about 12" to 18" high, to guard against damp and vermin, the latter chiefly in the form of

box perches

nesting boxes

dowelling or
fine mesh
partitions

A basic loft for performing pigeons. The interior *(Above)* is divided into three separate compartments, either by small-mesh netting or, as here, by wooden dowelling which is safer for the birds. Nest boxes should ideally be removable. Perches need to be constructed to suit the breed of pigeon kept. Equally, the size of the loft must be related to the number of pigeons which are to be housed. An arrangement of these dimensions and a height of 7 ft maximum from floor to ceiling would be suitable for 15–18 pairs. Keep the construction simple so that it is easy to keep clean and hygienic.

rats which, if given the chance, will burrow and gnaw their way into the loft attracted not so much by the pigeons themselves as by the scent of their food. In the front of each section there should be a weather-proof and pest-proof (mice will squeeze in at such places unless you are careful) ventilation inlet, about 9" square, set at floor level. Additional inlets can also be set in the end walls. A series of outlets 2'–3' long and 2" deep in the front and back, at ceiling height, complete the ventilation system. Stout but finely meshed wire netting provides a satisfactory lining for both inlets and outlets.

When partitioning and fitting out your loft you will naturally look for ways to make the most of available space. One important saving can be gained by incorporating sliding doors in the partitions. The partitions themselves may be made of netting, but all-timber divisions, using lath or the more expensive dowel, are better, as birds can damage themselves on wire netting, unless the mesh is very fine.

Perches are the next consideration and as these are your birds' day-to-day furniture it is important that they are well-constructed. Particular care should be taken to see that there are no sharp corners and also that the perches are positioned so that they do not jut out into the more widely used air-space. The type and size of perch you install will depend to an extent on the breed of pigeon you propose to keep. A conventional set of box perches, multiple units

Box perches of "pigeon-hole" type, suitable for Racing Homers.

of perches of "pigeon-hole" type (10" to 11" square, 5" deep), is ideal for Racing Homers but for show birds such as the high-standing Pouters, elaborately muffed Swallows and Trumpeters, or for Fantails, a more open perch is necessary, or else your birds will damage themselves or sully their plumage. There are many types of open perch, from a simple L-shelf to the more elaborate, but more satisfactory because more open, inverted-V. Bar perches with dropping boards are also effective. Hygiene is of prime importance and a periodic "spring clean" in addition to regular scraping out is advisable. For this a smart foray with the blow-lamp or gas torch as a back-up to the scraper is most effective, though be careful to keep the flame moving, or you might find yourself calling on the fire brigade.

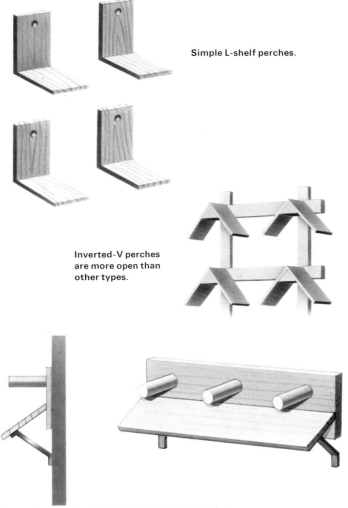

Simple L-shelf perches.

Inverted-V perches are more open than other types.

Peg perches with a sloping board to catch droppings.

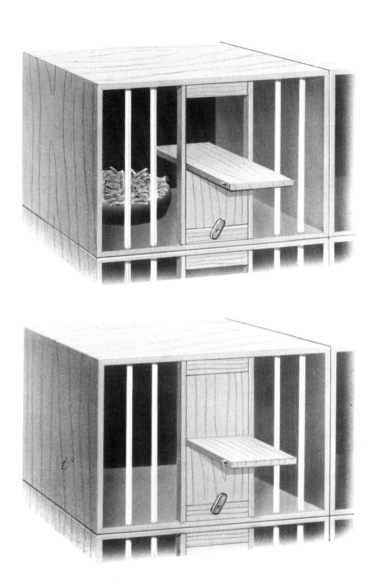

Nesting boxes should ideally have fronts of $\frac{1}{4}$ in dowel bars spaced $1\frac{1}{2}$ in apart. When closed, the T-shaped, pivoting door provides a spare perch. Either a nesting bowl or two house bricks, placed at right-angles across the corner of the box, should be provided as a base for the nest.

Nest-boxes should ideally be temporary fixtures that can be removed section by section, given a thorough clean and stored through the off-season. But provided they are built with a view to easy cleaning, there is no reason why they should not remain in place, unless, that is, you are pressed for room. The nest-box should, like a microcosm of the loft, be a roomy well-ventilated structure. Such breeds as Carriers and Pouters require special quarters, but for the Racing Homer you need a box with a floor area 24" × 18" and about 18" in height. There are several forms of nest-box front. If you intend to have a range of fixed boxes, a simple lath front (allowing not more than $1\frac{1}{2}$" between the bars) with a protruding landing area at the entrance is satisfactory. During pairing and in the off-season the entrance can be barred with a board that can be blocked into place. The landing area can serve as a perch during the off-season. Dowel front units with a T-shaped entrance designed to pivot to provide a closed front with exterior perch, or an open front with through landing board, are perhaps better than the lath type, as they are easier to work with and afford the birds greater privacy. To get the best from your pigeons during the breeding season, they must be made to feel secure. The nest box is their private territory – the rest of the loft they share according to the pecking order – and they need to feel it. It sometimes pays to erect a shielding board to screen the nest from view but whereas this might prove helpful in individual cases, it is not generally necessary in a well-managed loft.

Last, but far from least, there is the loft front, an area in which each fancier comes in time to devise his own combination of open-work, shuttering, "window-boxing," landing board and trap, or in the case of non-performing show breeds, aviary. The most important consideration here is security, against the weather, and against such menaces as prowling cats. To tackle the one you need only arm yourself with as much shuttering as you have open front, given that is that you have constructed your landing and entrance area on weather-proof lines. Against cats, there is no certain remedy but, if you wish to exercise your birds in your absence, you should take care to leave none but pigeon-sized access available.

As far as pigeon racing is concerned, a good loft is one that encourages quick trapping. The design of the loft front and exterior plays an important part here. There should be a minimum of distracting features: the landing area should be plainly visible, and so the roof should ideally slope forward, thus giving birds that land on the roof a view of the landing area they would not otherwise have and a relatively easy walk down to it. Roof-landings are sometimes discouraged by placing "fences" round the roof edge.

Traps come in many different forms, but the bob-wire and the frame are the commonest. Bob-wires are simply wires set at 1" to $1\frac{1}{2}$" intervals along a rail inside the loft so that they hang down over the mouth of the entrance. When a bird pushes against the wires from the outside, they give way and the bird enters. As it passes through the wires fall back into place, preventing the bird's escape. The frame trap can be constructed from wire or from timber and consists simply of a series of narrow drop holes: the bird can drop in through the holes but, as it must have its wings closed in order to pass through, cannot return the same way. Both types of trap should be detachable. Some fanciers prefer to use what is known as the "open door" method of flying their birds. As the term implies, this consists simply of leaving part of the loft front open and allowing the birds to enter unimpeded, and so of course to leave, if they should choose. For such a system to work well the fancier must have an excellent relationship with his birds, and when this is the case, the open door method is clearly the ideal one.

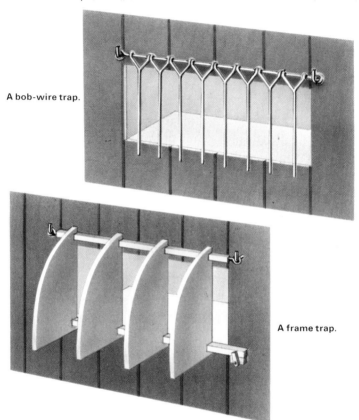

A bob-wire trap.

A frame trap.

Aviaries are only really necessary where fancy breeds too delicate for performance are kept. Then the aviary is of vital importance as it lets the birds come directly into the air and sun while protecting them from extremes of wind and possible bad weather. The aviary should be of good size, ideally sufficient to double the loft area and so allow for full exercise, and requires a sheltered aspect. A fine mesh netting will prevent undue feather damage and will also keep out pilfering birds which might otherwise add considerably to your food bills.

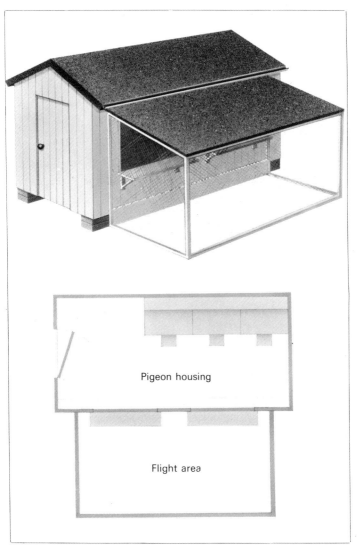

Pigeon housing

Flight area

Fancy breeds can be kept in a loft similar to that suggested for performing pigeons but if they are too delicate to be allowed out for exercise, which in general they are, they must have a good-sized aviary sited to provide plenty of fresh air and sunshine, while protecting the birds from very strong wind and rough weather.

31

Food and feeding

Domestic pigeons are essentially grain eaters. They will appreciate a little green stuff (particularly during the molt) and while foraging pick up a wide range of tit-bits, including worms, snails and grubs But the basic diet is made up of grain. Standard feeds on the market consist of various blends of peas, beans and maize or corn. Other small grains, including millet, wheat and rice, are generally used only sparingly, as stimulants prior to and during the breeding season, and when birds are to be pepped up for showing, when hemp or linseed can also be given in very moderate amounts. The beginner will generally settle for the best standard mix he can afford and work from there, the exact ratio of one grain to another being a somewhat academic issue at this stage. As may be seen from city strays and ferals, pigeons can get by on a pretty frugal diet if needs be. An ordinary standard feed from a reputable dealer, provided it is kept dry, will serve very well to begin with. Some breeds, such as Owls and other short-faced types, are, however, too small in the gullet to swallow beans and the larger peas. If you are planning to set up to breed short-faces you must seek advice on the best available feed – this will probably consist of small peas with tares, with millet and rice or wheat in the breeding season.

Feeding methods vary according to the type of pigeons kept and the time of year. For fancy or strictly non-flying breeds it is best to feed from a hopper, with food fairly constantly available. Performing pigeons require a feeding routine, the discipline of which is part and parcel of their training. They come to await the rattle of corn at a certain point in the afternoon and can be called in with ease, provided that this is the only feed they receive during the day. The food can be thrown broadcast onto the loft floor or else placed in hoppers. Loose feeding tends to reduce the number of squabbles, which can be quite numerous and troublesome after a cold day when the birds have taken exercise and are ravenous.

A grit hopper with a shallow tray and a storage section from which the grit can be dispensed. Alternatively, grit may be sprinkled daily on the clean floor of the loft.

A water fountain may consist of a simple lantern shape with vertical bars to prevent the pigeons from dirtying it and a roof to prevent fouling from above. It may have its own bowl or be open bottomed and placed over a bowl of matched size.

To keep your birds in good trim and, incidentally, yourself the more in pocket, it is important not to overfeed. Overfed birds simply become sluggish, in which respect they are just like their masters. Of the various ways of striking the right quantity of food to lay out each day, the most successful is by measuring an excessive quantity of corn into a hopper and allowing the birds to eat their fill. Whatever quantity remains should be subtracted from the original feed and then a further reduction of about a quarter of the total should be made. You can easily find out if your rationing is too meagre by feeling the crop of each bird after it has gone to roost. During a cold snap it is as well to be a little more liberal, and in the breeding season a plentiful supply should be available, for once there are young to be fed the general energy requirement is very greatly increased. Extra rations are also necessary for performing birds, once the season opens.

For the first few days of their lives young pigeons are fed with what is called pigeons' milk. This is a curd-like secretion from the lining of the crop of adult pigeons. The nestling puts its beak into the parent bird's mouth and takes the milk as it is regurgitated, in a pumping action by the parent. Production of pigeons' milk is controlled by the pituitary hormone prolactin. Later, partially digested food is passed to the young in a similar manner. Water should always be in good supply, not least, of course, in hot weather and when the birds are feeding young. Pigeons drink in a manner which, for birds, is highly distinctive. Instead of immersing the beak and then lifting the head to tip the water down the throat as most other species of birds do, pigeons drink by sucking, and so keep the beak immersed throughout. Drinkers should be of the standard type, having a good depth; they should be cleaned and refilled each day.

Other dietary requirements include various proprietary minerals and tonics (cod liver oil is a useful additive during the winter), but the most important item so far unmentioned is grit, which pigeons take to aid their digestion. Grain-eating birds such as pigeons have large crops in which their food is first stored and macerated. From the crop, having been mixed with peptic enzymes in the proventriculus, the food passes through to the muscular gizzard where it is ground up. The gizzard has a hard lining and contains numerous pieces of

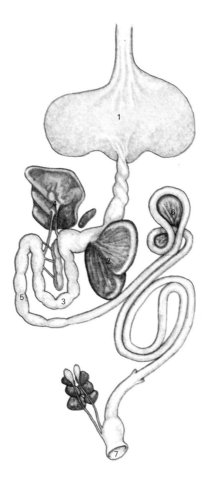

The pigeon's digestive system. Food is first stored and softened in the crop (1) and then passes to the gizzard (2) where it is ground by the grit which the pigeon has swallowed before it continues through the other digestive organs, (3) intestine, (4) kidney, (5) intestine, (6) pancreas, (7) cloaca.

grit. These form the cutting edges to the pigeon's corn mill. It is essential to provide pigeons with green stuff as regularly as possible, particularly where they are not flying out regularly. Lettuce is very good for this purpose and though expensive if bought at the greengrocer's can be grown in a small border from a relatively inexpensive packet of seed and without much trouble.

One last point to remember, apart from the need to keep grains dry and free from contamination by vermin or mold, is that sudden changes in diet can be extremely harmful. If you intend to add some of the smaller grains around breeding time or to introduce green food as the summer draws on, you should only do so little by little.

Pigeons appreciate being able to take a bath in cold water, especially if they are able to rest in the sun afterwards to dry. The bath should be about 3 in deep and should have a flange or ledge around it on which the birds can perch. It should not be left in the loft but put in about once a week to enable the pigeons to use it and then removed for cleaning out.

Ailments and their treatment

Prevention is always better than cure and, fortunately, pigeons which have been well tended, given the correct food and kept under clean conditions seldom suffer serious ailments. Avoid breeding from birds that have been seriously ill, or from birds which did not progress as they should have done when youngsters, and also from pigeons not fully developed. In all these cases youngsters are likely to be sickly. It may sound unkind but it is far better that a seriously sick bird should die rather than survive and propagate more illness. Extra care should be given at the time of the molt, as the strain upon the system is greater than at any other time.

Pigeons suffer from minor ailments such as colds: the symptoms, as with humans, are runny eyes and nose and sneezing; one-eyed cold, as the name suggests, is easily detected as the eye is closed. The bird should be isolated to prevent the complaint spreading, kept warm and treated with one of the many proprietary remedies. Canker of the throat is recognized by the appearance of a yellow cheesey growth in the mouth and throat, which if not soon treated will eventually choke the bird to death. There is now a satisfactory proprietary remedy for this complaint also. Any pigeon seen to be out of condition with its `head drawn in and body feathers fluffed out, should be isolated and observed. Unfortunately, clean and healthy pigeons sometimes come into contact with infections when in race panniers or show pens at an exhibition. It is, therefore, advisable to examine carefully any pigeon which has returned from a race or show and to isolate it from other birds if there is any doubt. Pigeons which have sustained apparently serious injuries from colliding with telephone or electricity cables or from being shot will, surprisingly, often recover without any serious after effects and assistance sought from a fellow fancier will often avoid the necessity of calling a veterinary surgeon.

Pigeons are subject to attack by lice, which either suck their blood or eat away their feathers, even when kept under ideal conditions. Fortunately these pests are easily erradicated by use of one of the several insecticides produced especially for the purpose.

A squab taking pigeon ''milk''
from its parent's beak.

BREEDING & REARING

Lᴇꜰᴛ ᴛᴏ themselves pigeons will form strong pair-bonds and will breed through the year, provided, that is, they have sufficient food and provided the winter weather is not too severe for too long. This is the natural way with dovecote and feral pigeons. From the fancier's point of view it is too random an arrangement. What he must do is introduce order to the dove house. He must arrange things, as the Victorians arranged marriages, to have the best of all possible advantages for his family. He might hope to breed a team of invincible racing or highflying birds, or a line of the most perfectly-structured and finely-plumaged pigeons that ever stood in a show-pen. To do so he will need not so much a breeding policy, for that is something he can only grope towards at first, but more a basic procedure to follow in early spring when the song birds are staking out their territories in hedgerow and garden, or, in a mild year, already nesting.

The first step, segregating the sexes, will in fact have been taken, in some cases at the end of fall, in others around the new year. Opinions differ as to the best time. On the one hand it is said that pigeons pair more readily after only a brief separation; on the other, there are problems involved in managing a mixed loft over a long period and these might be thought to outweigh the advantages of a more eager pairing. Either way the period of separation helps to dissolve the pair bonds established in the previous season, thus leaving the widest range of stock permutations open for the fancier to explore. From this point of view, the earlier you segregate, the better. Where pigeons have been paired for two or more seasons the bond can be extremely difficult to break, particularly within the same loft. It is in such cases that the third compartment of your loft proves its worth, for you can arrange to keep your old partners as far from each other as possible. If you do not have a mate for both the cock and hen concerned it is wisest not to attempt to break up the old pair. A free, unpaired hen will cause little difficulty, but an unpaired cock can be a positive nuisance.

Although some fanciers believe in pairing their birds before winter has properly ended, it would be unwise for the beginner to start so early. A sudden snap of cold weather can set things back in the pigeon loft just as it can in the garden, and chilled eggs or frozen chicks make a disappointing start for anyone. It is as well to wait until it is really Spring. If you plan to race in this first year (given that your birds are broken in) then matters are complicated by the molt. The problems it creates for the racing man are dealt with in the chapter on Pigeon Flying.

Having decided upon and recorded your pairings it is time to take your cock birds and post each one into a nest-box, closing the front and leaving each with food and drink for an afternoon and a night. In the morning, let each bird out to explore the loft on his own, closing him back into his new domain as and when he returns to inspect it. By this process the cock establishes himself in the nest-box. When you come next to introduce his mate, she will be more submissive than if she had been given first claim to the territory. In the latter case, particularly if she has been paired before, the hen will invariably create a great, violent fuss, pecking her proposed new mate and beating him with her wing butts. There will be resistance anyway, no matter what method of introduction you employ, but the shortest route to successful pairing is by establishing the cock first. Once you have slipped the hen into the box and the birds have settled, let each pair out by turn, as you did with the cocks, and allow the birds to come and go at the nest-box.

The cock bird will court the hen, inflating his crop and cooing strongly, sweeping his tail across the floor and circling round his mate, barely giving her a moment's peace. Bill kissing, in which the cock regurgitates food into the hen's beak, will shortly follow and after a series of circling and bowing movements and deep, sustained cooing from the cock, who will also indulge in frequent back preening, the hen will squat and the cock mount her. The pair may then be allowed out to celebrate, as it were, which they will do in the typical display flight, with wing clapping and sustained glides. Once you have seen all your birds settled in this way, you are then safely embarked on your first breeding season.

There will, of course, be problems. One of the trickiest for the beginner lies in the odd case of mistaken identity. In pigeons, the sexes are very much alike in appearance; there are no obvious points of identification. Cocks are generally more thickset with fuller heads and deeper keels. In hens the two bones at the vent are generally set wider apart than in cock birds but comparison can fail to help where what you are dealing with may well turn out to be either a large hen or a small cock, or two of either. The only true proof of a pair lies in the production of young, not simply of eggs, as paired hens will lay and attempt to incubate, sometimes with four eggs, which gives the game away, sometimes with two. The discovery that he has been keeping a hopeful eye on a false pair can be exasperating indeed for the novice who has set himself up with but two pigeons, but fortunately, in nine cases out of ten, the sexes are readily distinguishable from their behavior together, if not immediately from their appearance.

With your pairs established you need to instal nest bowls. These can be lined with wood shavings and a few bits of straw. An additional supply of building material – straw and twigs – should be left somewhere convenient for the birds to draw from as they wish, an activity they generally like, but must not be allowed to go too far in, as some birds will go to absurd extremes of construction given the opportunity. Earthenware bowls provide the best cup

Pigeon courtship is quite elaborate and often tender. The cock bird pursues the hen remorselessly, blowing out his chest and sweeping the ground with his tail. During bill kissing he regurgitates food into the hen's beak. Eventually after much cooing, driving and back-preening the hen will squat and the cock bird will mount and tread her.

for the nest, but two bricks placed at right-angles across a corner of the nest box will also serve.

A cock bird generally behaves with more urgency about nesting than does a hen. He will tend to occupy the nest for prolonged periods and sit complaining to the hen. If she wanders off, he will pursue her and urge her towards the nest, sometimes pecking at her sharply. Once the hen accepts the nest, you can generally expect the first egg in a day or two. In all this will be about a week, give or take a day, after mating has taken place. Pigeons typically lay two eggs. The first is generally laid in the afternoon and the hen usually stands over it, off and on, for an intervening day until laying again around noontime. Incubation begins with the arrival of the second egg, but it is not intense at this early stage and you should not worry too much to find the eggs unattended for a short period. Within a day or two, the birds will have settled down in earnest. Cocks share the incubation, sitting through the day from late morning to early evening. You should record the date of laying and from the date of the second egg you can allow 16 to 17 days before the chicks hatch. This period is a trying one for your pigeons, though not as trying as when they are feeding young, and you ought to do all you can to keep them fit and well. Both birds should have an opportunity to exercise as much as they want when off duty. A small feeder should be set up either within the nest-box

The newly emerged chick should leave a neatly opened shell.

(some fanciers use a small tin can) or hooked onto the outside. Food should also be readily available in a hopper or tray on the floor. It is while sitting that pigeons are prone to develop ticks and ailments resulting from inaction, which is why freedom to exercise is so important. If the weather is warm a bath should be provided and kept fresh, though if you are making an early start when the weather is still cold, baths are, of course, out of the question.

Another point of importance at this time is the need to maintain a settled and quiet atmosphere. Do not bring unfamiliar visitors to the loft and do not disturb brooding birds in order to inspect the eggs or to clean up. There is usually a spell when the birds change shifts in which you can take a look to see that all is well, and particularly to see that the surface of the egg is not contaminated with droppings. As incubation progresses, the birds will be increasingly reluctant to stir from the eggs. Then, on the appropriate day, the hatch will occur. Be sure to see that it is a clean one, that the small blind young are well formed and healthy-looking. The parents should, on a good hatch, clear the neatly halved egg shell from the nest. It should be clean on the inside without blood traces. In the event of a chick being deformed or sickly it is best to remove it immediately.

The growth of the young is remarkably rapid. Each day you visit the loft you will see a marked change as the young absorb more and more of the pigeon's milk which the parent birds pump into them (see the chapter on Food and Feeding). After five days the eyes open and within two more days the quill covering will have thickened up through the yellow down. It is now, with seven days behind them, time for the young birds to be ringed, a simple business but one requiring a gentle, firm touch. The ring is slid over the first three front toes of the right foot and up the leg until it has cleared the hind toe (illustrated on page 42). You should remember to put the ring on the right way up, so that reading it is straightforward. Ringing is important as it is the only way to assert your ownership of a pigeon and it is also a prerequisite of any form of racing or showing. By joining any of the pigeon clubs or societies you can obtain an annual issue of rings. The rings are dated and thus establish a bird's age.

It is important that ringing is carried out at this age and not left until the squab grows bigger. If ringing is delayed it will almost inevitably result in causing the pigeon pain and damaging the scales on the leg.

The young squeakers will grow stronger and more confident all the time, until, at around 17 days old they will be shouldering each other for room in the nest bowl. The pigeon loft will resound with their cries as their parents approach and the bustle and general commotion will be quite remarkable.

By now the young will have been receiving solid food from their parents for over a week and it is essential that you should see that water is readily available to the parents and that they are passing it on to the youngsters. Fairly large amounts of water are needed if the young are to digest their food comfortably.

The next step on the way is weaning. Begin this when the youngsters are clearly beginning to assert their independence. You will find them wandering

At seven days old it is time to ring the young squabs. This is done by sliding the ring up over the first three toes of the right foot and on up the leg until it has cleared the hind toe. It is an operation requiring a firm but delicate touch. For the rest of its life the ring will be evidence of the ownership of the pigeon.

a little from the nest bowl, though still pestering their weary and worn parents for food. It is now that the third loft section comes into full use. As many youngsters as are ready should be transferred to the spare compartment. Supply a food mixture in which all the grains are of moderate size, that is keep it free of beans, and provide plenty of water. Then be as vigilant as you can to see which birds are backward and losing out on the food. The safest test is to feel the crop of each bird at the end of the day. Where you find an underfed bird, it will be necessary to force feed. This can be done quite simply by holding the beak open with thumb and forefinger and pushing in individual grains. It is wise to soak some feed in advance so as to soften it up and assist digestion. An old method is to take a small mouthful of corn yourself and feed grain by grain from your mouth, using your saliva to soften the feed. Weaners can be taught to drink quite simply by dipping their heads into the drinker.

42

With racing birds or other performing types, the sooner you bring the young pigeons out into the air the better. To help them to orient themselves and gain a feel of their home it is useful to build a small coop that will sit over the landing board outside the young bird section. You can then, given fine weather, put the youngsters out to look at the world. The next step will be flight training.

PIGEON FLYING

OF ALL THE forms of pigeon fancying, keeping pigeons to race is by far the most popular. Although Racing Pigeons are highly bred, highly specialized birds, there is something natural about the sport that widens its appeal beyond that of any other branch of the fancy.

The basis of pigeon racing is, of course, the domestic pigeon's ability to "home," a talent, still largely unexplained, that man has put to use since ancient times, particularly in wartime, when pigeons have often proved invaluable as message bearers. We tend to think that this ability of the pigeon to fly home over hundreds of unknown miles is quite exclusive. But it isn't. All birds are able to navigate to some extent, and many do so with even greater long-range, pin-point accuracy than the domestic pigeon. Where they differ is in that they won't do it to order. An albatross might sweep its way half-way round the world to nest in the same spot on some small Pacific island, year after year. But homing pigeons are eager (if not always able) to return home at all seasons, at all times of the day or night, fair weather or foul.

To reach home pigeons draw on several "navigational aids," ranging from the sun's light and the earth's magnetic field to local landmarks. Their system is not infallible. Pigeons released in poor weather might be able to orient themselves, but then fall short on stamina. A certain percentage will simply prove not to have what it takes to survive in competition, returning home days after the event, if at all. Humane as it is to rescue an exhausted race bird and, by tracing the number on its ring, return it to its owner, in nine cases out of ten the lost bird will not be welcomed home, for it will have proved itself not worth its keep. Pigeon men are generally unsentimental in this respect.

As in any other form of sport, the participants in pigeon races need their training. The instinct to home is there, as is the ability to fly hard, but these need careful nurturing. It is no use sending a young bird off on a 500 mile race just out of the blue. That would be a disastrous course to take and an almost certain way of depleting your stock of all new promise. The first rule is to break your birds in gradually. Prior to their first training "toss" you should be sure they have spent enough time in the training basket, so that it is familiar to them and not a source of anxiety. An anxious jumpy pigeon is hardly likely to perform well. The young birds will have already spent some time weathering, taking in the view from the loft front during the weaning period. Flight training should be an extension of this, the first tosses being strictly local affairs of about three or four miles. You should train along the race path used by your local club, because this helps to build up the birds' knowledge of relevant local landmarks. Pick a day when the weather is good, even when training over such short distances, and if possible arrange for someone to release the birds for you, so that you can be at the loft to see how they return, in what order and general fashion. As the birds appear it is important to call or whistle to them, rattling some corn in a can, or employing whatever procedure you generally use at feeding time. This encourages pigeons to trap directly, even after such a short distance; though they will only do so with any style if you have kept them hungry beforehand. Step up the training flights little by little to 10 miles and on to 50 and 60, but don't by any means subject the pigeons to a crash program. By this time you will have found out where something of the promise lies, which birds are consistent, eager performers, and which appear to be laggards. But don't jump the gun. Some birds take longer to mature than others. There will always be surprises and in time you will find that while one bird is good over a short distance, another turns out to have the stamina for long distance racing. A good bird can be upset by so many things, it is impossible to list them. The safest advice is to stick to your routine, treat the birds gently and sympathetically, and so enable them to build up their confidence. Training birds singly is also useful, if not always practicable, for it helps to make for self-reliance. The training sessions for old birds will be more rigorous, but as with the young birds, moderation in training is vital.

A major consideration as the race season approaches is the molt. This is controlled hormonally and also genetically and its commencement cannot be accurately predicted. It varies, sometimes by a couple of months, from bird to bird, depending to an extent on the individual's date of birth. In general, however, an unmated pigeon begins to shed its all-important flight feathers in early summer. Paired birds used for breeding will begin to cast their flight feathers mid-way through a second incubation period. Bearing this in mind you should study the race program and plan your breeding accordingly, either to have your birds molt early, or late, or else to stagger the molt through the loft so you have your specialist fliers ready at the appropriate time. When starting out, of course, such foresight is difficult to apply and, indeed, there will always be problems. A sound rule, however, is only to enter birds that have their full complement of flight feathers and are not on the brink of casting their first flights. Each pigeon has its own quirks. One will perform best over middle distances when driving to eggs, another will race hardest over a short stretch when chasing a hen, while a third might cover 1,000 miles at record speed simply in obedience to its homing instinct. A method favored by the Belgians, who may be said to be the fathers of pigeon racing, is that known as widowhood. By this system a cock bird is encouraged to consume itself with jealousy for a hen to which it has been briefly paired. The anxiety that goes with separation is heightened, when the cock in question is allowed a final glimpse of his supposed mate in the company of another male. Widowhood is said to be a most efficient system, but it is as yet not widely practiced in Britain or the US. Only experience will tell you how to gain the best from your birds.

Some pigeon clubs operate mobile lofts with separate housing for each bird which can be used for a mass release at the beginning of a race. In pigeon racing it is not the first bird home that wins first prize but the one with the highest velocity – the greatest distance per minute – calculated by dividing the distance from the race's starting point to the loft by the time the pigeon took. Special rubber rings are issued for each race which are placed on the pigeon's leg.

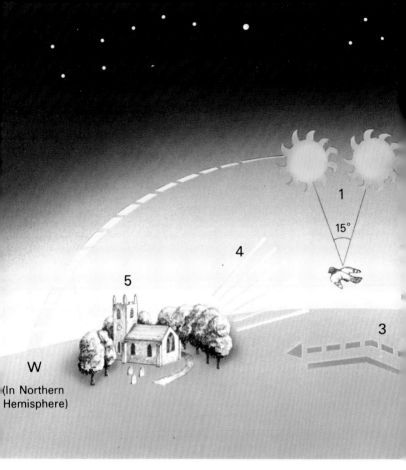

W

(In Northern
Hemisphere)

How do pigeons navigate ? We cannot pretend to fully understand how the "homing" ability of the pigeon works but scientific studies of pigeons suggest that some or all of the "navigational aids" shown in this diagram play a part. The diagram shows a northern hemisphere location.

1 The Sun used as a compass to determine orientation in terms of North to South and East to West position. This hypothesis assumes that pigeons have some kind of internal clock to compensate for the changing position of the sun (15° per hour). Under cloudy conditions there is some evidence that sunlight reflected from a patch of blue sky can be used, even if the sun itself is obscured. This hypothesis assumes that the pigeon has an ability to detect planes of polarized light – a skill already shown to exist in honeybees.

2 The Earth's magnetic field used to determine position. This hypothesis assumes that the pigeon has an interpretative ability not found in other animals.

3 Inertial guidance used. This hypothesis assumes the ability to remember

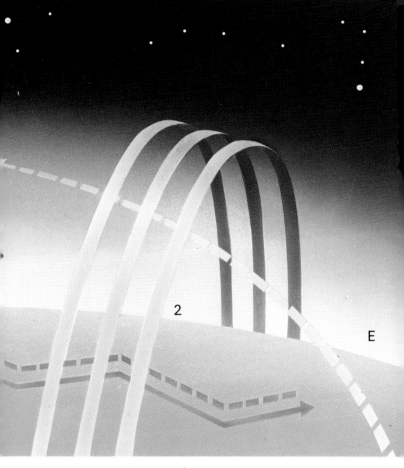

changes of course during the outward journey and to repeat them in reverse during the homeward journey. There is little evidence to support this theory.

4 Navigation by olfactory information. This hypothesis assumes that the pigeon has a sophisticated recognition of smells and smell gradients – as has been shown to exist in salmon. There is little evidence to support this theory.

5 Recognition of landmarks to guide navigation. There is little evidence to suggest that this comes into use except during the last few hundred yards of the journey.

6 Pressure pattern used. This hypothesis assumes an ability to recognize small changes in barometric pressure. There is some evidence to suggest that pigeons are able to do this.

7 Navigation by recognition of stellar positions. This hypothesis assumes that the pigeon has an internal clock and can correct visual information for celestial rotation.

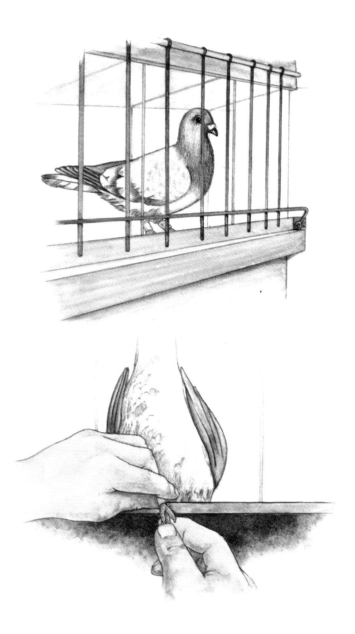

50

Each case must be considered on its merits, which means that the fancier has to be patient and appreciate that he is not dealing with a set of homing robots but with sensitive creatures whose true abilities can be set back perhaps more easily than they can be brought on.

Prior to a race, birds are taken to the club headquarters or rendezvous point where their rubber race rings are fitted and, in most clubs, their wings stamped with the club's address. Race clocks, the precision instruments that measure a bird's flight time, are checked and sealed. A race clock is an expensive but necessary item. If you keep your birds on a site where there are other lofts, you might reach an understanding with a neighbor by which you can use his clock to time your birds. But the process of running from one loft to another can not only waste valuable seconds, it can also threaten the success of your neighbors — you might just scare off an opponent's potential winner. On the day itself, your loft should be kept closed. Free-flying birds are nothing but a menace to all concerned on such occasions. Similarly you should warn all likely visitors to either arrive early if they must or not at all. As your bird begins to grow on the horizon, and then with wings crooked stoops down to your loft, the last thing you want is for him to be distracted by anything unfamiliar. All must be as he left it.

One point should be added : if the race is middle or long distance, be sure to feed your entrants before basketing. Pigeons home better when hungry, but cannot of course do well if weak with hunger. There is always the possibility of an appointed liberation time being postponed and the birds being held over unexpectedly.

(Information on the development of the Racing Homer is contained in Section D of the Guide under the entry Homer. Details of the sport of highflying are to be found in the same section under the entries on Rollers, Tipplers and Highfliers.)

A pigeon returning from a race enters the stall but is prevented by a locking bar from going into the loft. The fancier can reach in to remove the rubber race ring which is then put into the race clock making it register the time as that of the pigeon's arrival. The locking bar is then released and the pigeon can enter the loft.

PIGEON SHOWING

PIGEON SOCIETIES have been holding exhibitions for more than two hundred years. The first English society which can be traced with any certainty was founded in 1720 for the exhibition of the Carrier, the Pouter and the Almond Tumbler. The first pigeon shows in the US are believed to have been staged in 1873. Today shows are held in many countries and attract a big following. The British Pigeon Show Societies' annual show, at which no prize money is offered, attracted 3,690 entries in 537 classes in 1975 and in the same year the Young Pigeon and Poultry show in Hanover, Germany, drew 6,000 pigeon entries with a further 1,500 turned away in order to keep to single tier penning. Every two years the Federation Colombophile Internationale (International Pigeon Federation) holds a show – the Olympiad of the pigeon world – in which 26 different countries are represented. In this competition the pigeons have to fulfil specific racing qualifications and they are indeed the "cream" of pigeondom.

There is far more to showing a pigeon than just popping it into a show pen and collecting the prize afterwards. The effort involved in the exhibition side of the pigeon fancy has its own rewards but they are seldom monetary ones. The prestige gained usually far outweighs the prize money or the "pots." To be a good showman there are several essential factors which must be taken into account.

Showing gives racing men the opportunity of getting together during the non-racing season and for the showman to put forward the results of his season's breeding. Receiving a card for an exhibit you have not bred yourself never gives the same feeling of satisfaction as the "stormer" produced in your own loft.

Before showing, the exhibitor must be a member of the appropriate association or society; the birds must be wearing the correct rings and also be registered in the name of the exhibitor. The sight of a really good specimen, well prepared and exhibited in first class condition is a real delight for any fancier, but to reach that pinnacle it takes a great deal of time and patience and the disappointments are probably more than most would care to admit.

So, where and how do you start – first it would be advisable to visit as many local shows as possible, which will help you to interpret the standards for the various breeds and invariably you will meet someone only too willing to offer advice. (As written on the bottle — treat with caution.) Having established what is required to win, you attempt to breed to that standard.

Training for showing obviously will vary for certain breeds (for example, Fantails and Pouters require different treatment), but in the main similar principles apply to all pigeons.

Training should begin shortly after the youngsters begin to fly (around six weeks). They should be introduced to the show pen for intervals of ten minutes to half an hour at a time, and every week or two when convenient. A judging stick should be used to get the birds to pose correctly in the pen, but always with great care to avoid frightening the bird. A judge wants the pigeon to stand still in order that he can carefully weigh up its good and bad points and this is not possible if the bird is frightened or untrained.

In addition to pen training, attention must be given to those special points required in the various breeds; for example, the tail of the Fantail; the beak and ceres of the Dragoon; the wattles of the Carrier and Barb; the foot feathers of Trumpeters and Swallows and the "blowing" of the Pouters, to mention but a few. Advice on such attention would need to be sought from an expert on the particular variety or from specialist literature.

All show birds should be shut in, even flying varieties during the show season, and kept on clean dry sawdust; which must be cleaned regularly to remove droppings. Above all, keep the pigeons away from damp as their feathers soon pick up moisture and start to deteriorate. Handle your birds frequently, smooth out and replace any feathers which may have become disarranged through the pigeon cleaning itself; or as a result of some accident. This smoothing out is done by holding the feather between the thumb and forefinger — don't grip the feather too lightly or you will pull it from its socket.

Examine your birds carefully for any signs of feather lice, for these will not be tolerated by any judge, and for a fancier to exhibit a pigeon which is lousy only shows that he has not bothered and does not deserve to win. There are many good insecticides on the market which will completely eradicate this pest, so there is really no excuse.

Many fanciers add a little linseed to the diet of their show birds to put that additional finish to the condition of the feathers.

Before despatching pigeons to a show, be sure that all the feathers are dry; that the basket is also dry with a good layer of coarse sawdust covering the bottom. (Fine sawdust from hardwood gets damp very quickly and will often stain the feathers, especially of white birds.) Make sure that the feet are clean and that the ring numbers are readable. So many, otherwise good exhibits are spoilt by dirty feet.

If you are able to take your birds to the show and pen them yourself, so much the better. But generally speaking, if you have to send them unaccompanied, they are usually well looked after by highly responsible stewards on arrival at the show.

It is rarely necessary to wash a bird, especially if it has been kept as previously mentioned, but if you find that it has to be done, it is not such a delicate task as may at first be considered. You need to be gentle but firm.

Pigeons may be held against the body or against the forearm but should not be held by the wings. The pigeon's feet should be placed side by side between the first and second fingers with the wings folded naturally at its sides and the thumb covering the primary flight feathers as far as possible. The other hand can then be placed against the breast to balance the bird. By pivoting the pigeon's body to rest against the forearm the pigeon can be carried comfortably.

The other essentials are a fine and preferably warm sunny day, and three bowls. The operation should take place in the morning after the pigeon has had a light feed. The first bowl should contain warm soapy water; the second bowl clean warm water to which glycerine has been added (the quantity should be about one teaspoonful to one and a quarter litres of water) and the third bowl clean water which has been slightly "blued" with the old fashioned laundry blue.

Take the pigeon firmly in the hand; soak the wings and tail and with the aid of a small sponge rub out towards the end of the feather until the natural color has returned. It is now time to start on the head, neck and remainder of the'body. Great care must be taken to avoid soap getting into the bird's eyes; we all know how uncomfortable that can be. Having removed all the dirt it is now necessary to remove the soap, taking care not to damage the webbing of the feathers.

Give the pigeon a good rinsing in the second bowl and then a quick final rinse in the third. Plenty of water must be used for rinsing. It is absolutely essential to remove all traces of soap as it will give the feathers a rough appearance when dry.

Now remove all the surplus water by drawing the wing and tail feathers through the thumb and finger. Mop the body with a dry sponge absorbing as much of the water as possible, and finish by wrapping the pigeon in a soft dry cloth. It may be necessary to repeat the last performance. The bird should then be placed in a pen in the sun, out of the wind and allowed to dry off naturally. If the day should be cold, the operation should take place as near the heat source as possible – remembering that, as the pigeon dries the heat should be reduced so that it is acclimatized before being returned to the loft or pen.

Washing should be carried out at least a week prior to showing to allow the bloom to return to the feathers.

PIGEON TOPOGRAPHY AND OTHER FEATURES

These illustrations will help the reader to identify structural and other points, types of marking and styles of feather development in the typical domestic pigeon. Like the illustrations in the Guide itself they show an ideal state, the state which every fancier tries to achieve.

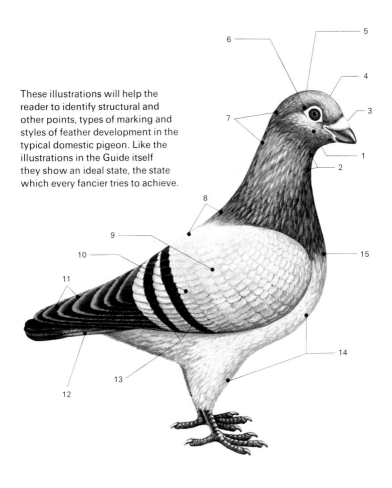

TOPOGRAPHY OF THE PIGEON. 1. Cheek 2. Bib 3. Wattle 4. Frontal 5. Crown 6. Eyecere 7. Nape 8. Saddle 9. Coverts 10. Middle Coverts 11. Wing Flights 12. Rectrices 13. Wing bars 14. Breast 15. Crop

Long face

Medium face

Down face

Short face

Muffed

Slippered

Groused

FACE AND FEET TYPES

Badge mark

Beard mark

Baldhead

Spot

Helmet

HEAD MARKS

Shell crest

Peak crest

Double crest

Hood

Breast frill

Rose mark

FEATHER TYPES

60

BREED
GUIDE

A: WATTLE, RUNT AND TABLE PIGEONS

This grouping embraces the large, wattled pigeons of Middle Eastern origin; the large Runt pigeons, and other assorted breeds of above average size. The latter consist of birds that are or, until relatively recently, were bred primarily for the table. Some of the larger Homer varieties are also used for this purpose. These are treated in the section on Performing Pigeons and Related Varieties.

BAGDAD

This is an important strain of Syrian origin which has been influential in the development of a number of breeds, and appears in several varieties.

The **French Bagdad** is an unusually rangy bird with long legs and an exceedingly long neck. Head and beak are the most telling features. The head should be flat and long, forming a straight line with the beak, which must also be long. Rounded heads are the commonest fault in the French Bagdad and should be avoided. The eye is marked by fine cere and there is only a slight beak wattle. This minimal wattling is unrepresentative of the strain as a whole. The variety has been important in the formation of the Maltese (below) and the Magpie (Section C).

The **Nuremberg Bagdad or Scandaroon** is a rangy bird noted for its unusual beak. One of its German names translates as the "crooked beaked" Bagdad. The important points are in the head and beak and the line they form between them. The head is narrow and very arched and its tight curve must continue in the beak. The wattle is moderate, sometimes having a pinkish tinge, and should help fill out the arched line of the head. The beak is flesh-colored. An even cere is required.

Scandaroons are bred in pied and colored forms; in the pieds, a neat patch of color at the base of the beak and back to the eye is considered a good point. Feathering is hard and compact.

The **Steinheimer Bagdad**, another German variety, is not unlike the Scandaroon. It has a long, if not so markedly curved beak. This pigeon has long wings and tail, but its legs are much shorter than those of the Carrier and Scandaroon. It is more or less limited to Germany and is not even widely kept there, although its size makes it a worthwhile proposition as a table bird. Other varieties include the **Batavian Bagdad**, the **Great-Wattled Bagdad** and a **Bagdad-Mondain** cross. There are also some central European varieties about which little has been recorded.

During the 19th century, Bagdads were used in perfecting the closely-related Carrier (below).

French Bagdad

Nuremberg Bagdad
or Scandaroon

Steinheimer Bagdad

63

ENGLISH CARRIER

The English Carrier is an unusually tall pigeon famous for its large, cauliflower-like wattle. It has been developed in Britain for more than 200 years, has close affinities with the Bagdads (above) and the Barb (below), and is believed to have played a part (the exact extent is nowhere agreed upon) in the creation of the Dragoon (below). It is popularly thought of as the message carrying breed but, although it might at some stage have been used as a messenger, it is certainly not used as such today, being strictly an exhibition pigeon. Charles Darwin wrote of the Carrier of the mid-19th century that it was "too valuable" to be flown.

Fanciers have concentrated on the development of the head, beak and wattle, and the proportions of these features are of the utmost importance. The Carrier is long-faced and narrow-skulled, the bead being flat. A line from beak tip to pupil should measure about $2\frac{1}{4}$in in cock birds and not less than 2in in hens. The beak must be sturdy throughout its length and should appear to pierce right through the middle of the wattle. In profile the wattle is rounded, while from above it has a slightly oval look. Tightness and evenness are the hallmarks of a good quality wattle, as is a fine white coloring. The cere forms a full white circle about the typically red eye. Ideally the center of the cere should be diamond-shaped.

The Carrier neck is narrow and long, adding considerable height to the already rangy body. Legs are long and the feet stout. Overall length should be between $17\frac{1}{2}$ and $18\frac{1}{2}$ inches. The Carrier is very close-feathered. This, together with its length, makes it look slimmer than it really is. It is a broad-chested variety and should weigh between 20oz and 23oz. Blacks, blue bars, duns, reds, yellows, whites and pieds are bred.

BARB

This heavily wattled breed, is generally accepted as being closely related to the Carrier (above). This relationship is not immediately apparent, both because of the difference in size, the Barb being overall a lot smaller than its cousin, and the difference in beak length. But the Barb has been referred to before now as a "short-beaked Carrier" and the breed of the 19th century is recorded as being significantly longer-beaked than the present-day version.

The Barb is among the oldest of pigeon breeds. Its name, or, more particularly, the now obsolete Barbary, suggests a North African origin, but there is no hard evidence, and indeed the Barb's relationship to the Carrier (and so to the Bagdad strain) tends to refute such a theory. A Middle Eastern origin is thus probable.

As is self-evident, head, beak and wattle are the major features. The skull should be broad and squarish, and the beak, though short, should be thick both vertically and horizontally. The wattle should not conceal the beak, but it should be full and neat. In old birds wattling tends to run somewhat to seed and this, combined with the short beak, can lead to rearing problems. Other birds should therefore be kept for fostering the young. The cere or eye wattle

Red Carrier

Black Carrier

Black Barb

Yellow Barb

65

should be full and clearly defined, forming clean-edged red circles about the eyes. In combination with the beak wattle they must serve to emphasize the square and broad look of the head. For their size, about typical pigeon size, Barbs have large heads. The legs are clean and shortish. Although the Barb has a low carriage, its general appearance is bright and alert. Barbs come traditionally in blacks and duns, though pieds occur, and yellow and white forms are also bred. The Barb takes three to four years to develop fully. It is a pure breed and all attempts at outcrosses come to nothing in the long run.

DRAGOON

The Dragoon, formerly known as the Dragon, is an English show pigeon of powerful build, also a good utility breed. The Dragoon has been bred in Britain for more than 200 years – Birmingham and London each for a time having rival versions – and in the US since the 1890s. Its popularity was highest in the late 19th century; more recently it has tended to lose ground to the Show Homers (Section D) and, in the US, to the Carneaux and the Kings (below). It has been used to give strength and body to the Genuine Homer (Section D) and also to commercially bred squabbing homers.

The breed seems to have evolved from a Carrier (above) and Pouter cross (Section B). There is disagreement as to the role played by the Carrier; some think the Dragoon may have descended from the Horseman.

The Dragoon is a bird of strong and noble looks described as being "like a guardsman on parade." Its beak is not only impressively sturdy but also unusual in that the upper and lower parts are of the same length and size. The beak is held well up, which, together with the slightly-rounded and broad skull, tends to give the Dragoon a nose-in-the-air look, a feature further emphasized by the white "nose band" of wattle. Another important point is the damson eye cere. In body the Dragoon is wedge-like. The feathering is hard and short.

White Barb

Blue Dragoon

Red Checker Dragoon

RUNT

The name Runt is given to several varieties of large pigeon, bred primarily for the table but also kept as show birds. Runts of 48oz are not uncommon, which, in weight terms, puts them on a par with domestic chickens. The term "runt" has been used indiscriminately in the past to denote any large bird of otherwise conventional pigeon type, particularly the offspring of crosses between dovecote pigeons and larger breeds such as Carriers and Dragoons. This practice has resulted in confusion, making it difficult to trace the history of the breed. True Runts have however been bred in Italy, France and Spain for more than two centuries. There are German and English common Runt varieties, and in the US the Giant American Runt has been developed.

The **Italian or Leghorn Runt** has a long, bowed neck, short legs, and a stout beak that is medium to short in length. Wattling is never extensive in the Leghorn. The body is thick-set, a feature emphasized by the erect tail carriage. Attempts have often been made to improve or to develop new breeds through Runt crosses but these seldom pay off. An exception is the Leghorn cross used in the creation of the Florentine (Section C). The **French or Roman Runt** and the conventional **Spanish Runt** are closely related to the Leghorn. Crested Runts and Runts with feathered feet are also bred in Spain where the most striking native variety is surely the now rare **Flamenca Runt**. It has an extensive red cere (up to 1in in diamerer) which is heavily carunculated. The beak is short and heavily wattled. The throat bulges out under the lower mandible and is almost bare of feathers at this point. These features (except for the latter) are reminiscent of the Barb (above), as is the Flamenca's low carriage.

In the **Giant American Runt** we have a popular table variety which continues to gain ground as a show-bird. Its main features are the full head, cobbish neck and heavy, deep shoulder. Runts generally tend to be loose-feathered but the Giant's plumage is hard and close. The wings are short and are carried with the flights above the tail. Giants have been used in developing the King (below) and there have been crosses with Homer varieties.

Runts are bred in most color varieties. They tend to fly little, being such heavy birds, adapted to their role as squab producers.

Spanish Runt

Flamenca Runt

Blue-barred Common Runt

Red Giant American Runt

69

MONTAUBAN

A French breed of large, crested pigeon, the Montauban is believed to be the result of a French Runt-Mondain cross. A number of factors point to such an origin. The Montauban is loose-feathered, like the French Runt, and bears a crest, as do some of the larger Mondain varieties. Size is another pointer. Montaubans commonly weigh over 32oz. At that weight they are intermediate between the Runts and the squabbing Homers. The breed was used in the US to develop the Giant American Crest, a Mondain variety (below). The extensive shell crest is the Montauban's most distinctive feature. This completely encircles the back of the head. The eye is white with a black pupil; the beak horn-colored. Montaubans are bred in blacks, reds, yellows, whites and mottles.

CARNEAU

The Carneau is a table and exhibition pigeon first developed in northern France and southern Belgium, and a popular breed in the US. Derived from the French Mondain and feral stock, it was originally a utility bird, a role for which it is ideally suited, being a prolific and easily-managed type whose squabs quickly fatten to the 16oz mark. Carneaux can weigh above 36oz, though 22–32oz is a more reasonable weight range and one from which show birds should be drawn.

When breeding Carneaux for the show room the main features, apart from size and weight, are color, carriage and head. Reds and yellows are the traditional colors, but in the US, where much has been done to build up the weight of the breed, solid blacks and duns are bred; there are rosewinged and splashed forms also. Solid, rich color, with a good penetration to the downy part of the feathers is important. A fine neck sheen is a further mark of quality. The plumage itself should be tight.

The ideal Carneau carries itself in something of a proud, upright manner, high on its legs and with the head well up. Overall it should be a bird of strong, broad lines, deep-keeled, full in the shoulder and with a strong yet graceful neck. The Carneau head is particularly distinctive, having a high domed front, and being broad between the eyes, with a sturdy medium-lengthed beak surmounted by a fine cream or pinkish wattle. The beak should be light in color, except in the Black Carneau, in which it should be dark.

A delicate red cere lines the eye, emphasizing its prominence; in the black form the cere can be black to coral. The largish eye is orange in color. Flights are carried over the tail, crossing about an inch above its tip. The tail itself is broad and squarish.

Red Carneau

Montauban

White Carneau

Black Carneau

71

KING

The King is a table and exhibition pigeon developed in the US in the past 50 years. Runt, Mondain, Maltese and Homer strains are the breed's basic ingredients. Kings are characteristically short-bodied, thick-necked birds, commonly weighing up to 36oz. They occur in the following color varieties, in all of which short, heavy birds are favored.

The **White King** is one of the breed's most popular color varieties. Important features are a sturdy pinkish-white beak surmounted by a medium wattle, and a well-rounded head. Head-size is important: the skull should be sufficiently large to balance the general bulk of this typically broad pigeon. The ideal type measures about 5in across the breast. The eye should be prominent and dark brown – almost black – in color, and should be offset by a delicate beet red cere. Legs and feet are beet red. Plumage should be firm and totally unblemished.

The **Silver King** was bred from silver varieties of the basic crosses referred to above. The Silver King has a horn-colored beak surmounted by a whitish wattle. Ideally the eye should be pearl with contrasting beet red, finely-drawn cere. Legs are beet red. Plumage color is the major factor. Wings should be silver, barred with black-brown. Back, rump and tail should be deep silver. Plumage is dark at the head, becoming lighter down the slightly lustered neck until at the breast it is as nearly the same color as the wings as possible. The tail is barred.

In the **Blue King** variety marking is similar to that of the Silver; the basic color is a striking sky-blue. The beak is blue-black and the eyes are orange, surrounded by the finely-drawn red cere typical of the breed.

Other colors: Black, dun, red and yellow Kings are also bred. Colors should be strong and unblemished. The orange eye, beet red cere and shanks, and horn coloring in the beak are common to all varieties grouped here, except the black, in which the beak is dark.

POLISH LYNX

Poland's table pigeon, descended from common pigeon stock, is a medium-sized pigeon, not, in terms of weight, a competitor with the other table breeds of this section (apart from the Strasser, below). A cross upon the Pouter (Section B) is thought to have been important in forming the breed – at least this is how some authorities account for the Lynx's full-breasted appearance, and also for its coloration.

The Lynx is bred in spangled and barred forms, chiefly in blues and blacks. The bird's head and body are usually dark, shading off down the bird's length. In the spangled forms the basically light-colored coverts are heavily laced. Barring is white, edged or laced with color. The primaries are also white. Red and yellow Lynxes are bred but they are not common.

White King

Silver King

Red King

Polish Lynx

73

STRASSER

The Strasser is an Austrian table pigeon which, like the Polish Lynx (above), was developed from field pigeon stock, in this case through crosses with the Florentine (Section C). It is not an ideal table bird, lacking the size of modern squabbing breeds. The Strasser is bred, on a small scale, in the US, where it has been profitably outcrossed upon the King (above), to increase its size. It is a distinctively marked pigeon which will in all probability go the way of the Florentine and the Coburg Lark (Section C) and become increasingly a bird of the show room – if it survives at all in its present form.

The plumage pattern derives from that of the Gazzi Modena (Section C) through the Florentine. Strassers are bred in blacks, blues, reds, yellows and whites. The head and upper bib are colored, as are the wings, back (an unusual feature, distinguishing the Strasser from its cousins) and tail. The body plumage is white. Barred and barless forms predominate, the latter being particularly attractive. Laced varieties are also bred. Strassers with white primaries were once common. The present-day breed has a more upright carriage than earlier versions, a feature particularly evident in King outcrosses.

MONDAIN

There are several types of Mondain, all heavily-built Runt-like pigeons originating in Italy and France, and bred in those countries and in the US, where some distinct varieties have been developed. All tend to be prolific, efficient squabbing varieties. They are bred in plain-headed, shell-crested and clean- and feather-legged forms. Carriage is typically low. The more common Mondains come within the 20–36oz weight range. Their influence upon table breeds is considerable. They were instrumental in the development of the King (above).

Italian Mondains. Three varieties predominate here; all go over the 32oz mark. The **Romagnoli Mondain** is a short-winged, short-tailed variety. It is broad in the breast and generally typical of the breed. Romagnolis are bred in grouse-legged and muffed forms and in all colors. The **Sottobanca Mondain** is a shell-crested variety. Its general conformation resembles that of the Romagnoli: short in wing and tail, and low-slung. It is also bred in the full range of colors. The **Piacentini Mondain** is a white variety, longer from head to tip of tail and more like a common Runt, than the other Italian Mondains dealt with here. It may have served at some point in the development of the Swiss Mondain.

French Mondains. Most important among the French varieties, and one of France's oldest breeds, is the attractive **Cauchois Mondain**. The Cauchois is medium-sized, weighing 22–26oz, and has a more upright carriage than do other Mondains. A large crop and beautiful feathering are further distinctions. They suggest that Pouter stock (Section B) has contributed to the evolution of the Cauchois. Color variation is remarkable. Laces are bred in hyacinth, red, yellow and white. Blacks, blues, reds, silvers and yellows are bred and there are red, yellow and white barred forms. Individual

Blue-barred Strasser

Red White-barred Strasser

Romagnoli Mondain

Sottobanca Mondain

75

feathers are often multi-colored. There is a distinctive white bib, like a small shirt front, on the finest Cauchois. The Cauchois is an above average squab producer. This fact, together with its beautiful appearance, make it an extremely attractive proposition.

The common **French Mondain** is a more ordinary pigeon, probably derived from the Italian Romagnoli. A plain-headed, clean-legged variety, it is a squat, short-bodied bird in the 24–32oz range. The **Mondain of Picardy** is unusual in being a peak-crested Mondain. In other respects it closely resembles the Carneau (above), as the red plumage immediately suggests, and is probably the product of a Carneau-field pigeon cross. It is one of the smaller Mondains, weighing around 18–20oz.

American Mondains. Several Mondain varieties of great interest have been developed in the US. The picture is not a clear one, for early on the name Mondain, as happened to an extent with that of Runt, was applied rather indiscriminately to large squabbing birds of low carriage. The **White Swiss Mondain** (the Swiss connection is not at all clear) is a major variety, weighing 36–40oz. Like the Italian Piacentini, the White Swiss is a longer bird than the common Mondain type. It is generally a more graceful pigeon too. This is a matter of proportion and carriage. The White Swiss is in fact broad in the skull and breast and stout-necked. Wings are strong and held close to the body, the primaries carried up above the tail. The overall impression is of a well-tailored bird of forward carriage which stands firmly, its feet well apart. Dark brown eyes are surrounded by a nice red cere; the bill is white with a small pink-to-white wattle. Plumage should be pure white with a silvery sheen on the neck.

The **Jewel Mondain** is a more recent US variety, used both as a show and a table bird. It is a heavy pigeon, with individuals over 32oz common. The Jewel is the product of several crosses within the Mondain breed, including White Swiss, Piacentini and French. It occurs chiefly in grizzles. The **American Duchess** is an early US Mondain variety, somewhat resembling the Romagnoli. It is a large pigeon and one that is heavily muffed, not an ideal combination from the squab breeder's point of view. It occurs in white only and is now extremely rare. US fanciers have created their own **American-French Mondain** out of a combination of Mondain varieties. The American-French Mondain is a thickset bird of typical Mondain appearance (not unlike the Jewel).

Another, more impressive creation is the **Giant American Crest**. This appears to have developed initially almost as a by-product of the American-French. The latter is plain-headed, but it once came in crested types. Although there is no hard information on the subject, it is thought that these crested birds formed the basis of the Giant American Crest. The variety is a bulky one, birds of 32oz being standard and heavier specimens occurring quite commonly. It is straight-backed and carries itself well, with the wings held close, the flights above the tail. The crest is of the shell type, and of moderate length. There is something of the Carneau (above) about the variety. An unusual experiment to produce a miniature, approximately half-size, American Crest has been undertaken with some success. The **Minia-**

Cauchois Mondain

French Mondain

White Swiss Mondain

American Duchess

77

ture American Crest, as the end-product is known, is quite a good likeness of the Giant but the proportions are not yet exact. The Miniature is not a common fancy. It is bred for the show room in whites, reds and almonds.

MALTESE

The Maltese is a stilt-legged breed with a long goose-like neck, a compact body which resembles that of common domestic fowl and a sharply elevated tail. The origin of this unusual pigeon is not clear. It has no known connection with the island for which it is apparently named. A form of Maltese was bred in Germany in the mid-19th century which is believed to have derived from an Asian breed (characterized by its elevated tail) imported into Italy in the 17th century.

Today's Maltese is thought to be the result of a cross between the German variety and the French Bagdad (above). The latter's influence may be seen in the length of neck and leg (a similar influence is evident in the Magpie, Section C). Originally the Maltese, like the Fantail (Section B), lacked an oil gland, but this is not the case today. Maltese pigeons should stand around 15in. Tail elevation, a short compact body with hard feathering, and slender neck and legs are important guides to quality. Wings must be tucked up well, following the line of the tail. The head should be plain, beak wattle and cere unobtrusive. Black, blue, dun, red, white and yellow types are bred.

The Maltese played a major part in developing the King (above) but is itself too rangy to be a practical proposition for the squab breeder. It is now strictly an exhibition breed.

Giant American Crest

Black Maltese

Blue Maltese

B: FEATHER AND DISPLAY PIGEONS

Pigeons noted for their distinctive feathering have been assembled here together with those, like the Fantail and the Pouter, in which a highly elaborate display has been evolved. It is not an exhaustive coverage but one that is reasonably representative of what has been achieved in both areas as a result of careful selection.

FANTAIL

A major, ancient breed of fancy pigeon, which originated in India or China, the Fantail is a bird of fascinating appearance and behavior. It has been most highly developed in Western Europe and in the US. In Britain, for a period during the last century, there were two distinct schools of Fantail breeding, the Scottish and the English. The Scots tended to neglect the tail to concentrate on carriage, while the opposite was true of the English who, in addition, went in for a wide-spread tail, held forward and almost flat across the back. The Scottish, with its smart carriage and motion, was closer to the modern bird. Fantails are sometimes referred to as "shakers" because of their unusual convulsive movements when excited. The Broad-tailed Shaker was an early English Fantail variety. For reasons that need no explanation, Fantails are also sometimes called "peacock pigeons."

The number of feathers in a "fan tail" varies considerably (usually about 30–32; sometimes as many as 42) but fullness and stiffness are more important than quantity. However it is worth remembering that the Rock Dove *Columba livia* typically has 12 tail feathers and that 12 or 14 are the normal number in most domestic breeds. Fantails generally lack an oil gland.

Charles Darwin, discussing the breed's evolution, writes of being sent, "from Amoy in China, the skin of a Fantail belonging to a breed known to have been imported from Java. It was colored in a peculiar manner, unlike any other European Fantail; and, for a Fantail, had a remarkably short beak. Although a good bird of the kind, it had only 14 tail feathers . . . ." Darwin explains that specimens of this breed with 18 to 24 tail feathers were however on record, and continues, "From a rough sketch sent to me, it is evident that the tail is not so much expanded or so much upraised as in even second-rate European Fantails. It has a well-developed oil gland. Fantails were known in India . . . before the year 1600; and we may suspect that in the Java Fantail we see the breed in its earlier and less improved condition." The remainder of the breed's history, so far as it concerns us, has been one of improved display and greater plumage and color variation.

Red-saddled Fantail

Indian Fantail

White Fantail

Black-tailed Fantail

Present-day Fantails occur in a wide variety of forms. They are all extremely spry and energetic birds, right from the feather-legged **Indian Fantail**, a robust, shuttlecock of a bird, somewhat downfaced and bred in peak-crested forms, to the Lace or Silky Fantail with its whispy tail plumes.

Fantails are highly-strung pigeons. Their gait is cocky and strutting. General behaviour can be greatly agitated, marked by compulsive trembling. Yet for all this, the Fantail is notably tame and affectionate. Carriage of head and neck is an important feature. When the bird is displaying, the head should be held right back, so that it rests low down, almost at the base of the fan, forward vision being totally obscured. From the front a displaying Fantail should appear to have no head at all. The breast, generally broad, varies in degree of fullness, but is always well-rounded. Indeed the Fantail is a pigeon of full, curved lines. The spread fan should form a full circle.

Peak-crested and feather-legged types, still bred in Asia, were once fairly common in Europe and the US, where a peak-crested class, the **White Calcutta Fantail**, was developed for a time, but the trend has been away from that type of adornment to produce a plain-headed, clean-legged pigeon. Color range, on the other hand, has been widened considerably. Nearly everyone is familiar with the **White Fantail**, the form most commonly kept in garden dovecotes. There are, however, many different color varieties and several interesting combinations of marking. Among the most popular colors, apart from the whites, are the blacks, silvers, blues, yellows and reds. There are saddles and particularly attractive tail-marked varieties, such as whites with black tails, colored with white tails, and whites with only the outer edge of the tail colored.

The **Lace or Silky Fantail** is another interesting form, though by no means a modern development as might be imagined. Lace feathering is an abnormal condition in which the feathers have no barbs and so seem whispy and hair-like; it can occur in any breed from time to time. In a good Lace the silky feathering is restricted to the tail which, when fully extended, looks rather like a fretwork or fine tracery. All Fantails are limited in their powers of flight by their extensive tails. Lace Fantails, being at an even greater disadvantage, are relatively feeble fliers. This probably explains why they are not a popular fancy.

MOOKEE

The Mookee is a crested breed of Indian origin noted for its neck-trembling display which has close affinities with the Fantail (above). It is possible that the now extinct Narrow-tailed Shaker was an early form of the Mookee. Apart from the trembling or shaking display, the Mookee also resembles the Fantail in the way it arches back its neck. This is not done to the same extent as in the Fantail, but in general the stance, upright with the breast a full curve, is remarkably similar to that of the more famous breed.

The Mookee has a conventional pigeon tail. Its feathering and coloration are particularly interesting. The crown of the head is white, color breaking off cleanly above the peaked crest. In the best examples the beak reflects this

Powdered Silver Fantail

Silky or Lace Fantail

Ash-red Mookee

Black Mookee

83

sharp color demarcation, being two-toned: white above and dark below. The two outer flight feathers should be white. Mookees are bred in whites, but the colors are obviously more interesting. They come in duns and blacks and in blue and red barred forms.

JACOBIN

This highly unusual hooded pigeon is among our most ancient show breeds. Little is known of the Jacobin's origin and early history but it is generally held to have been introduced into Europe from India.

There are four important features: the hood of long feathers extending over the crown and in the modern Jacobin obscuring all but forward vision (they need to be trimmed back during breeding); the chain, a ruff or collar of less extensive feathers; the mane; and the rose of reversed feathers. It is the quality of the last two which decides the completeness of the Jacobin's feather-duster or bouffant look. The mane and rose were bred in during the 19th century. In the process something of the toy quality of the Jacobin, hitherto prized as one of the most diminutive of all domestic pigeon breeds, was sacrificed, much to the displeasure of some turn-of-the-century Jacobin enthusiasts.

The Jacobin has long been popular throughout Europe, particularly in Germany, where it was once known as the "wig" pigeon. It is also bred in the US. But it is a difficult breed to perfect and is therefore nowhere common. Black, blue-barred, red, silver, tigered, yellow and white varieties are bred. In all the colored varieties, the head should be white from a line just below the eye; the primaries and tail should also be white.

Beak-crested and muffed varieties have been produced but neither has proved to be very popular.

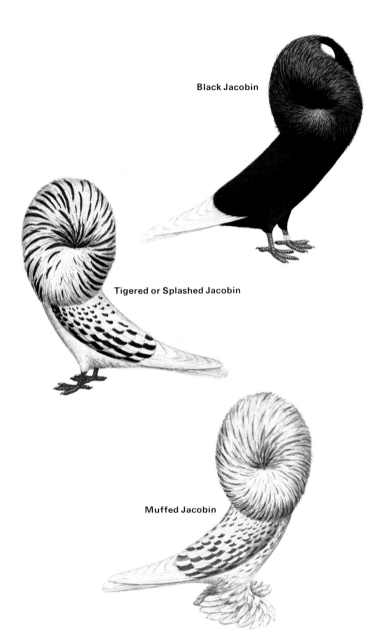

Black Jacobin

Tigered or Splashed Jacobin

Muffed Jacobin

85

TRUMPETER

The Trumpeter, a breed originally named for its distinctive voice, a rapidly repeated and sustained cooing, is now valued as a feather pigeon. In its feathering it is among the most elaborate of all domestic pigeon breeds. The Trumpeter, a bird of Asian origin, has been bred in the West for more than 200 years. Early authorities described it as a runtish breed. Like the typical Runt, it tends to be loose-feathered. The typical Trumpeter is muffed and crested, the extent and nature of these features differing considerably between its several varieties.

German fanciers have done most to develop the breed, both in feathering and color variation. Trumpeters are relatively rare outside Germany. They are difficult pigeons to keep and breed from. Prior to mating, muffs, under-feathers and, in the case of heavily feathered types, the rose must be trimmed back. Foster birds should be kept to hand.

The **English Trumpeter** is a shell-crested muffed pigeon. There is also a small crest of reversed feathers above the beak. Although they can be extensive the muffs on the English Trumpeter should only be of moderate length. In general its continental cousins, such as the **German Double-crested Trumpeter**, are more finely bred. The latter has extensive muffs: the feathers on both tarsi and feet being fully developed. It is shell-crested and has a short crest reversed over the beak. German Double-crests are bred in reds, yellows and whites, and in attractive mottled and white-barred varieties. The **Dresden Trumpeter** is similarly double-crested. Its reversed beak crest should be neat and round; it sometimes, incorrectly, extends a little beneath the beak. The Dresden is a white shield pigeon, that is, having white wing coverts. The **Bernberg Trumpeter** is similar to the Dresden in conformation and virtually its exact counterpart in marking: the head, muffs, primaries and tail are white while the body is colored. The **Erbsgelbe Trumpeter** is extensively muffed, lacks the shell crest, but has a neat beak crest.

The so-called **Russian or Bokhara Trumpeter** is the most highly bred of all the varieties. Its feathering is quite extraordinary. Rose and shell crest are fully developed. Its muffs spread out in wide fan shapes that are more extensive than in any other breed, except perhaps for the Spot (Section C) and the Swallow (below). A front view of a high quality Bokhara shows very little of the "pigeon" within the feathers. Bokharas are bred in many colors and patterns: solid blacks, whites and reds being most common.

Other varieties include plain-headed types, such as the **German Split-tail,** and a number of beak-crested birds, for example, the **Saxon, Vogtland** and **Altenberg Trumpeters**.

The "trumpeting" voice has now been almost entirely bred out.

English Trumpeter

German Double-crested Trumpeter

Dresden Trumpeter

Russian or Bokhara Trumpeter

87

SCHMALKALDEN MOORHEAD

The Schmalkalden Moorhead is an extremely attractive, ruffed breed of German origin, noted for both its feathering and marking. It is sometimes referred to as a Mane Pigeon. The major feature of the Schmalkalden is the full ruff which rings the upper neck so that the head appears to nestle in it. The head and bib are colored, as is the tail. The remainder of the bird, including the ruff and the extensive muffs, is white. Muffs cover the feet and tarsi well but are of moderate length.

SWALLOW

This German breed is noted for both its feathering and coloration. There are two main varieties which are sometimes treated as distinct breeds: the Swallow proper and the Fairy Swallow. Although they occur in plain-headed and clean-legged types (for example the flying variety known as the Thuringian Fairy Swallow), Swallows are best known as feather pigeons. The feather-legged Swallows are possibly the most extensively muffed of all domestic pigeons (see Trumpeter, above). Some varieties are also shell-crested, the crest encircling the back of the head from just under the eye. Swallows bear distinctive markings. The body and tail are white, the wings are colored and there is a small "cap" of color on the crown, or, in some cases, a color spot like a Cyclopian eye on the front of the head above the wattle. Muffs are also colored.

The Nuremberg Swallow is an old variety; it is shell-crested with a rosette on each side of the head. The plumage is all white except for the colored "cap" (fullhead), wings and muffs. The muffs are only moderately long. One feature deserves special notice: the Nuremberg has an unusual, long quill feather extending from each wing to the oil gland at the base of the tail. These quills appear to serve as oil ducts to assist preening. They account for the often oily or silky plumage of the Nuremberg.

The Saxon Fullhead Swallow is a shell-crested variety with a colored "cap" as the name implies and it has the typical Swallow markings. It is slightly smaller than the Nuremberg and is more extensively muffed. White-barred forms are particularly popular.

The Saxon Fairy Swallow is a shell-crested variety. The crest, which goes from ear to ear, is marked by a small rose at either side of the head. Muffing is long and extensive, the legs being fully booted.

The Double-crested Fairy Swallow is a rare Thuringian variety and near extinction. It is very close to the Saxon, but is distinguished from it by the reversed feathering above the beak, a feature found in the Trumpeter (above).

The Tiger or Bohemian Fairy Swallow has particularly extensive muffs and is also noted for its coloration: the flight feathers are alternately colored (two colors only, black or red) and white. This feature resulted from a cross upon a white shield Dresden Trumpeter (above). The bird is otherwise close to the Silesian Fairy Swallow (below). The tigering extends to the muff feathers, though there is no alternation. Some authorities claim that the Tiger

Schmalkalden Moorhead

Nuremberg Swallow

Silesian Full-head Swallow

Double-crested Fairy Swallow

89

Swallow's distinctive wing patterning can be achieved through selection alone; others say, that if the "wrong" feathers are drawn, the "right" will grow in their place.

The Silesian Fairy Swallow resembles the Saxon Fairy, but lacks crest and mane. It has the frontal head spot; "fullheads" do not occur in this variety.

The Thuringian Fairy Swallow is plain-headed and clean-legged and said to be a good flyer. **The Thuringian Swallow** is similar to the Nuremberg with a "fullhead" and shell crest, but the legs are clean.

Swallows are bred in a wide range of colors. Among the most attractive are the reds and the blacks, both spangled and tigered; the silver dun-barred; the white-barred blues, particularly where the bars are edged with black; the barless blue; the spangled blue; and some of the silver-laced varieties. Barring should be narrow and distinct. The white plumage should be absolutely clear of blemishes. Spot and other crown marking (fullhead) must have a clean outline.

PTARMIGAN

The Ptarmigan is an English muffed and crested variety, with lightly curled feathering on the back and on the wing coverts, said to resemble snowflakes. An all-white pigeon, it is a relatively new breed, having been produced in the 1920s by the then Hon. Pike Pease and named for the grouse-legged game bird, the Ptarmigan. The feather curl is reminiscent of that in the Frillback (p. 92) but is not as extensive. Ptarmigans are bred in plain-headed and crested types; crests can be either peak or shell. It is a well built bird, somewhat on the coarse side.

Ptarmigan

Red Tiger Swallow

Silesian Fairy Swallow

Black Barless Saxon Full-head Swallow

91

FRILLBACK

This exhibition pigeon is noted for its curled or frilled feathering from which its name derives. The Frillback is a fairly rare breed and little is known about it except that it is not of recent origin: 18th century European authorities refer to it as an import from Asia Minor. Today the breed has a following in Eastern Europe and in Italy, France, Germany, Britain and the US but is nowhere a particularly popular fancy. Frillbacks have been described as being Runt-like in shape; they are certainly larger birds than the typical Homer, but they are of the Homer rather than the Runt type.

Quality of feather is more or less the be-all and end-all of the Frillback. The frilling occurs on the outer wing coverts and the back and affects only the smaller top feathers. These are curled, hooked or ruffed. The effect should not be one of a bird that has been pulled backwards through a hedge: the frilling must be neat and always relatively tight and firm. Frillbacks come in plain-headed and shell-crested types and may be muffed or clean-legged. In the crested and muffed forms (particularly those with grizzled coloring) the frilled look is inevitably more complete, indeed the feathers of the muff are often hooked and curled too. Apart from grizzles, the Frillback is bred in whites (possibly the commonest form), creams, blacks, reds and blues. There are also barred types.

POUTER

This breed is comprised of several highly unusual varieties of balloon-cropped pigeons, some of which are known as Croppers. The breed is referred to by early 17th-century authorities and is certainly older, the Pouter or, as it was then known, the Cropper of the 1600s being already a well-developed specimen.

Crop inflation is a common feature among pigeons. In the Pouter it is carried to quite astonishing extremes — one is tempted to say that it goes almost to bursting point. The Pouter crop is the same as that in other domestic pigeons in all but size, although the diameter of the Pouter's upper esophagus or gullet is unusually large. Male Pouters inflate the crop more readily and more extensively than do females. Birds can be induced to inflate by blowing into the beak, but for showing they need careful training, a matter of drilling them and of exploiting the mutual interest between the sexes. When shown a hen bird, a male will naturally begin to display, and vice versa. The fancier must develop a system whereby the birds associate a call or signal with the imminent appearance of a member of the opposite sex. This can only be achieved with patience. Pouters will fly with the crop inflated; during such display flights they also strike the backs of their wings together to make a clapping sound. In general, the modern Pouter is a tall, long-legged, long-bodied and narrow-girthed pigeon. The English Pouter (below) stands around 16in high, being some 7in in the leg.

Today's Pouter is believed to have originated in Holland, where a number of interesting varieties have been bred for more than 300 years. The **Dutch**

White Frillback

Cream Frillback

Dutch Cropper or
Old Holland Pouter (Harlequin)

Holle or Amsterdam Balloon Cropper

93

Cropper or Old Holland Pouter exemplifies the major difference between the continental and English varieties in being a comparatively thickset bird. It is however this variety which many authorities consider to be the progenitor of the English Pouter (through the Horseman, which gave the latter length of feather). The Dutch Cropper is a muffed variety, long in the leg and erect of carriage. It is bred both with and without a crescent crop marking (ideally with) and comes in a wide range of colors. The inflated crop should be medium-sized and globe shaped.

The **Holle or Amsterdam Balloon Cropper** is a small pigeon. When displaying it is reminiscent of the Fantail (above), though it has only a short and normal tail and is very much more rounded in shape. The wings are also short. When standing the Holle Cropper should hold its tail parallel to the ground. In flight it holds its head up rather than forward. It is bred in a wide range of colors, pied varieties being common.

The **Slenker** is a rare Dutch variety of Pouter bred for flying rather than display. It is a small pigeon, with only a small crop display. The legs are short. In carriage it is again reminiscent of the Fantail. The Slenker tail is longer than that in the Holle, and is held downwards. Slenkers fly with great panache, spurting into the air with furious wing-beats and proceeding in a noisy clapping flight.

With the **Voorburg Shield Cropper** we come to a particularly attractive Dutch variety. It is a shield pigeon, that is, its wing coverts are colored. The Voorburg is a moderately tall bird of upright carriage. It is a more slender pigeon than many of the continental Pouters and has a fairly large crop which when inflated sits up well to cushion the beak. The tail is held just clear of the ground. This elegant pigeon, a fairly recent creation by the famous Dutch artist C. S. Th. van Gink, is bred in a wide range of colors, the barred varieties being particularly attractive.

Like Holland, Germany is an important center of Pouter breeding and there are several distinctive German varieties. Of these the **German Magpie Pouter**, a form of **Saxon Pouter**, is a large, long-legged muffed pigeon with typical magpie markings: colored crop, breast, nape, back and tail and an additional cap of color. Other German magpie Pouters are the **Bohemian Saddle** and the **Elster**, which is particularly smart in the isabel white-barred form. The **Silesian Pouter** is thought to have been first bred in what is now part of Czechoslovakia. It is a medium-sized short-legged bird noted for its sprightly appearance and full crop display. Colors and white-head varieties are bred, the former in blues and grizzles and reds, the latter in black, blue, red and checkers. Germany's equivalent of the English Pigmy Pouter (below) is the **Brunner Pouter**, a game-looking pigeon that also makes a good little flying bird. Crop inflation is moderate, in keeping with the bird's essentially practical lines. White-barred forms predominate.

The breed to contrast with the Brunner is the **Old German Cropper**, a heavy, short-legged bird, resembling the Dutch Cropper (above) but being clean-legged. The **Hana Pouter**, a bird of Czechoslovakian origin, is a tall, muffed variety bred in white with the head and upper crop (or bib), back, wings and tail colored. Other German varieties of note are the **Pomeranian**,

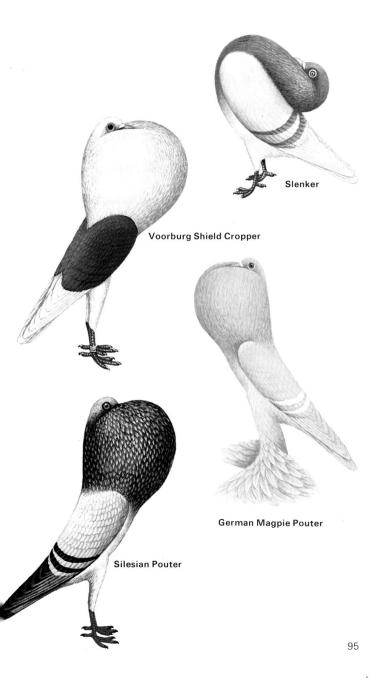

Slenker

Voorburg Shield Cropper

German Magpie Pouter

Silesian Pouter

Hessian, **Whitehead** and **Thuringian** (a peak crested variety).

While continental fanciers concentrated, as they so often do, upon color variation, the English went in for line and carriage, evolving some world famous Pouter varieties. They used the Horseman to add length to the Dutch stock, and quite frequent Runt crosses to add height, then selecting to reduce the consequent increase in girth.

The **English Pouter** is stilt-legged and slender of body. The crop inflates to a full round, cushioning the beak. In its color and marking, the English Pouter conforms to detailed standards, particularly regarding the pied markings. Basically, the bird is colored, with white flights and body (below a line approximately one third of the way down the keel), and white tail and legs. The crop has a distinctive crescent-shaped blaze of white and there is an interesting piece of white reversed feathering near the wing butts. Legs should be straight and narrow, even at the top. They should "enter" the body cleanly, without overlapping plumage or surplus weight. The feet should be lightly feathered, a quality achieved by selecting between the two extremes, playing one off against the other. The **Pigmy Pouter** is a diminutive version of the English Pouter, weighing about 10oz, approximately half the weight of

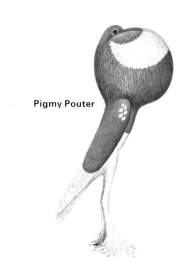

Pigmy Pouter

Black Brunner Pouter

Black Hana Pouter

Black Brunner Pouter
(crop deflated)

the larger variety. The **Norwich Cropper** is a medium-sized variety. Markings are similar to those of the English Pouter, but there is no mistaking the two varieties, for the Norwich is much the smaller. Similarly it is a sturdier bird than the Pigmy Pouter. It is bred in pied blacks, blues, reds, silvers and mealies. Outside London and also Scotland (a major Pouter region) the city of Norwich, Great Yarmouth and other East Anglian centers, played a vital part in the breed's evolution during the last century.

Among other interesting varieties are the German **Swing Pouter**, a flying variety of medium build, popular in some areas as a show bird, the **Spanish Marchenero Pouter**, a low-standing, small pigeon which is unusual in the way it holds its tail down in flight, and Spain's **Valenciana Pouter**, in which the crop is held well down. French Pouters include the **Amiens** (a clean-legged bird otherwise resembling the English Pouter) and the pigmy **Little Pouter**. The **Ghent**, a large pigeon related to the Dutch Cropper, and the **Boulant Signor** are bred in Belgium.

English Pouter

Norwich Cropper

Swing Pouter

White Marchenero Pouter

99

C: COLOR AND TOY PIGEONS

German Toy breeds form the basis of this section. They are all represented here, with the exception of the Swallow, which appears in the section on Feather and Display Pigeons. *Also included are other breeds noted for their color, feather and structure, among them the Oriental Frills and the Owls.*

MODENA

This Italian breed of some 150 color varieties, formerly a highflying breed, is named for the city of Modena. The breed may be traced back to the 14th century when it was used in a sport that might best be summed up as a form of pigeon piracy. A Modena flier, or *Triganiere*, trained his birds to fly to particular points above the city at the direction of a flag and to mix with the flocks of other fanciers. He then signalled for his flock to peel off and return, in the hope of luring away and bringing down for capture any pigeons foolish or feckless enough to be tempted away from their own flock or loft. This ancient sport is not exclusive to Modena, competitive highflying of the kind having been common in other cities, particularly in New York City (see Flight in Section D) and in Glasgow in Scotland.

The present-day Modena is a comparatively modern creation. In the 19th century the Modena lacked the full, rounded shape characteristic of today's breed although one authority records "almost countless" color varieties, "the rarest being most esteemed."

Body shape should be uniform throughout the wide range of colors. Modenas are short in the beak and have rounded heads, which they carry erect. Neck and breast are full and the body is solid and well-keeled. The tail should be carried horizontally, well up from the ground. Flights are a little shorter than the tail and are held neatly above it. To match this compact look, the Modena is suitably close-feathered. Wattling should be neat and unobtrusive. The breed is a hardy and active one, and makes a good parent. Modenas keep both fit and clean (given that they are properly housed) and are altogether a good breed for the newcomer to pigeon showing to take up with.

The sheer range of color varieties makes a full description too extensive a task for the present format. There are, however, two main groups of Modena: the **Gazzi**, a pied form, and the unpied **Schietti**. Marking in the Gazzi consists of white body with colored crown, face and upper bib, and colored wings and tail. The subvariety **Magnani** is simply a mottled form of either the Gazzi or the Schietti. The subvariety **Zarzanelli** is a rare form of Gazzi in which the

Bronze Gazzi Modena

Silver Gazzi Modena

Blue Schietti Modena

colors have a clouded appearance and are not so sharply demarcated from the white plumage.

Modenas are bred in all the known colors and may be barred, self, checkered or laced. The **Argent Modena** is a particularly striking variety. A sort of reversed Gazzi, it is distinguished by white shields or wing coverts that are finely laced throughout and set against a colored body. Barring can be most unusual in its detail, as for instance in the bronze-barred blue Gazzi. In the Schietti, the Magnani, with its mottled, harlequined and almond plumage forms, is possibly the most impressive. Schiettis are also bred in all-whites.

FLORENTINE

The Florentine, as the name implies is a breed of Italian origin. In markings and in general outline it resembles another, perhaps better known, Italian variety, the Gazzi Modena (above), from which it is partly derived. The Florentine is however a far larger, rangier bird than the Modena, a feature that points to the other important element in its make-up, the Leghorn Runt (Section A). Florentines are bred in Italy and in Germany, and also, on a small scale in the US. The Florentine was initially a table breed, enjoying great popularity as such as in the early part of this century, but, as befits its stylish appearance, it is also bred for exhibition. In fact the bird's value as a producer of large squabs is now somewhat overlooked.

Plain-headed and clean-legged, the Florentine stands well, its head erect and tail high. The wings, shortish with white primaries, are carried above the tail. As already mentioned, the markings are similar to those of the Gazzi Modena: the head and part of the bib are colored, as are the wings, except for the white flights, and tail. There is a good sheen to the bib. The head itself is nicely curved, the dark beak held down a little and surmounted by a medium white wattle. Florentines have played a part in the creation of that other attractive, rangy breed, the Hungarian (below). They come in the following colors: black, blue-barred, brown-barred, blue-checker, red, and yellow, each against a white ground plumage.

Magnani Modena

Blue-laced
Argent Modena

Blue Florentine

White-barred Florentine

HUNGARIAN

An attractive exhibition variety, the Hungarian was once used primarily as a squab producer in Eastern Europe, Austria and Germany. The modern Hungarian is an upright, broad-bodied and firmly-feathered pigeon. Its markings are most distinctive. Face and bib are colored. A thin line of white leads from the base of the bill up over the front skull. It then widens across the crown to form a cape. The bib of color comes to a point at the breast, leaving a clear streak of white between the breast and the wing butt. Primaries and thighs are white. The remainder of the bird is colored.

In a good Hungarian the line between white and coloured plumage is sharply defined – the more marked the contrast the better. The Hungarian of the mid-19th century was a less sturdy pigeon and tended to hold its tail down rather than in the neat, elevated style of the modern breed. A cross between the Florentine (above) and the Swallow (Section B) is believed to have laid the foundation for the breed. Hungarians are bred in blacks, reds, yellows, silvers, blue-bars and checkers.

MAGPIE

This interesting show breed, of Tumbler origin (see the long-faced continental Tumblers in Section D), is named for its "magpie" colouring and noted for its slender looks and elegant carriage. The Magpie was first bred in Germany and later imported into Britain in the second half of the 19th century. At that time Magpies had, in the words of one author, "ordinary Toy or Dovehouse pigeon heads, clean legs, and trim bodies, possessing no properties at all but colour and marking." From this description it is clear that radical changes must have been made at some point, and they were, when, in the early 1900s the slightly improved German form was outcrossed on the French Bagdad (Section A). The move revolutionized the breed, giving it the length and grace for which it is now chiefly valued. Head, face and beak should be fine and long and of even proportions, one important standard being the balance of the area between the back of the head and the beak tip. There should be three equal parts to this, marked out by the pupil, and by the base of the beak. The eye is pearl or white with a fine pink cere. The beak should be flesh-colored, with an unobtrusive wattle. Markings are as follows: head, neck, back tail and breast are colored, the remainder of the bird being white. Magpies generally reproduce true to type as far as marking is concerned but if any failings occur the fault can usually be remedied by selecting from birds in which the color keeps well up the breast. Black, blue, cream, dun, red, silver and yellow varieties are bred. The breed is highly strung and if not tended carefully, with regular handling, will become flighty and unmanageable.

Red Hungarian

Silver Hungarian

Black Magpie

Silver Magpie

MARTHAM

The Martham is a form of Magpie (above), but lacking the distinctive pied marking for which the latter is named. Marthams are not at all common. They evolved as a by-product when the early Magpie of German origin was improved by outcrossing on the French Bagdad (Section A). Blacks, creams, duns, reds, whites and yellows are bred and there are blue, silver and mealy barred types. Grizzles, checkers and laces also occur. The Martham was used in the development of the Show Flight (Section D).

ANTWERP SMERLE

Now a British exhibition breed, the Antwerp Smerle originated, as the name suggests, in Belgium. A white bird with colored wing coverts; its characteristic breast frill is reminiscent of the Turbit (below). The likeness is, however, only superficial, for the Smerle is an altogether larger, plain-headed pigeon of more conventional Homer type.

Ideally the Smerle is a sleek and smooth pigeon, with a tidy breast frill. The short beak (in Belgium the term "smerle" is commonly applied to short-beaked varieties) should complete the full curve of the head, and the dark eye should be rimmed by a fine flesh-colored cere. Reds, blacks, duns and yellows are bred and there are barred, checkered and laced varieties.

Antwerp Smerle

Yellow Magpie

Black Martham

TURBIT

The Turbit is a short-beaked, frilled breed, not unlike the Owl (below) in general characteristics but differing considerably in particulars. The Turbit has been bred since at least the mid-17th century, when it enjoyed a fair reputation as a flying bird. (It was later an ingredient in the development of the Belgian Homer, Section D.)

The present-day Turbit is radically different even from the breed of the last century, and this is largely due to the attention paid during the past 50 years to the formation of the head and beak. The Turbit head is full in the nose with some length of forehead, extending right over the short beak which, with its tight-fitting band of wattle to fill out the curve, does not protrude at all from the head. This gives the Turbit something of a reptilian look about the face. It also, incidentally, restricts the bird in the business of rearing young and so necessitates the use of foster birds. American fanciers stress the desirability of a full or long front skull.

Turbits are peak-crested and should have a neat supporting mane. The breast frill should be as extensive as can be achieved without producing anything loose or ragged. To achieve a high standard in all these points is particularly difficult. Marking is of the typical "turbit" type, namely white, but for colored shields. Turbits are bred in a wide range of colors and in barred types. Birds with colored tails are also sometimes seen.

ARCHANGEL

This toy pigeon is noted above all else for its highly iridescent plumage. The English name Archangel probably derives from the French word *arc-en-ciel* meaning "rainbow" although the breed is commonly associated not with France but with Germany, where it has been bred for more than 150 years and where its potential as a color pigeon has been most fully developed. Authorities differ as to the precise history of the breed, some claiming it comes from India or Persia, others that it is of Italian origin. Whatever the case, few support the idea that it could have an all-German ancestry. This may be explained by the fact that although the Archangel is generally classed as a toy pigeon, it is altogether a much more finely bred type than the average German toy, which tends to be somewhat loose-feathered.

The Archangel is a neat bird of slim line and upright posture. It is traditionally bred in either crested or plain-headed types, (a monk-headed variety has also been bred, in Germany). There are two color types: red and yellow, each in five combinations: black-winged; white-winged; blue-winged; black-winged with white flights; and blue-winged with white flights. All color combinations other than Red Black-winged Archangel are usually known by the name Gimpel. British and US fanciers prefer a crested form of the Red Black-winged, or Dark-bronze. They also breed the Yellow Black-winged Archangel, or Light-bronze. The all-important iridescence should be readily apparent over much of the plumage. Crests are of the peaked type and should ideally reach a very fine point.

Black Turbit

Blue Turbit

Blue-winged
Red Archangel

Yellow White Winged Archangel

109

ICE PIGEON

The Ice Pigeon is a German toy pigeon noted for its beautiful ice- or lavender-blue plumage. Bred in muffed and clean-legged varieties, it is of the typical dovecote pigeon type, short in the leg and plain-headed, and is valued exclusively for its color and marking. Ices occur in a wide variety of colors. The basic and original Ice is a pure lavender-blue self-colored bird. There are now barred and laced forms with dark flights and tails, and sometimes with barred tails. Varieties with spangled shields also occur. Some markings are especially delicate, particularly in the case of the white-barred blues, in which the barring is edged with black, the flights are blue-black and the tail is barred. In all there is a gradual shading from paler to darker blue down the length of the bird and the plumage has a powdery bloom. Ices are generally dark in the beak and the eye, although orange-eyed forms do occur. Muffing should be full and neat. In the cleaned-legged variety there are also black checkers known as Forellen.

ORIENTAL FRILL

A handsome Turkish breed of color pigeon introduced into Germany and Britain in the 1860s. The typical Oriental Frill is a peak-crested pigeon with a characteristic breast frill and groused legs and feet, although plain-headed Frills with clean feet and legs also occur. All are short-beaked and derive from the Turbit (above) and the Owl (below). In head shape they are closer to the Owls than to the Turbits, being more down-faced than the latter. They are particularly admired for their rich coloring and detailed marking. Three main groups exist: Satinettes, Blondinettes and Turbiteens, each with wide color variation.

Satinettes are basically white with colored coverts and tail. They have groused legs and feet and come in several patterns, the chief of which are as follows. **Bluette**, a white-barred blue with solid, light-blue coverts and dark blue tail. The bottom edge of each bar should be lined with black. **Blue laced**, a white-saddled type in which the saddle is laced with dark blue. Each of the feathers in the dark purple-blue tail has a distinct white spot or bar. **Silverette**, a silver-grey saddled bird with a tail of similar color. The wings are barred white, each bar being edged below with dark grey. **Silver laced**, equivalent of the Blue laced, with dark silver-grey lacing the saddle. **Brunette**, a tawny variety in which the tail and saddle lacing is of darker, reddish brown. **Sulphurette**, yellow-brown variety, otherwise resembling the Brunette. **Black laced** and **Dun laced**, are white-based with narrow lacing throughout wings and tail. **Vizor**, a blue helmet-marked bird in which the head, from the upper bib back to include the crest, is dark blue. It otherwise resembles the Bluette.

Blondinettes are colored, with no white except in the lacing and in the tail spot or band. They are marked in the same patterns as the Satinettes and occur in a wide range of colors. Black and dun laces and blue- and silver-barred varieties have spot tails. Others have the tail laced. Both Blondinettes and

Clean-legged Ice

Satinette

Muffed Ice

Silver Laced Blondinette

Satinettes should be bred in the same way, by pairing the lighter marked birds with those of heavier marking, and continually selecting for color. The potential of young birds is particularly difficult to judge in this case. It will be found, for example, that the tail spot often comes only with the first molt and that first plumages are quite confused in coloring and marking.

Turbiteens are turbit-marked, that is having a white body with colored shields. They are distinguished by their fine peaked crest and by the three marks of color, one on each cheek and one on the front skull. These marks should be regular and clearly defined, without any stray peppering or ticking. Colors include blacks, reds, duns and yellows, black-barred blues and black-and brown-barred silvers. All colors are noted for their unusual richness.

OWL

This ancient breed of frilled pigeon, named for its owl-like round head and short, down-turned beak, is closely related to the Turbit (above) and is probably of Asian origin. The Owl is one of the smallest of all domestic pigeon breeds. Resemblance to the Turbit has at times led to confusion, particularly during the last century, when some authorities contended that the Owl was merely a plain-headed, whole-colored Turbit. The differences are chiefly in the head and beak, and in the extent of the frill. The latter should be slightly rose-shaped and shorter and more compact than in the Turbit. Head, wattle, beak and gullet (which is filled out), should combine to form a complete curve. The beak is short and stout, the upper mandible coming down over the lower. The eye should stand out well, in keeping with the rounded form of the head, of which it should mark the central point.

There are two main Owl varieties, the English and the African. Different national varieties proliferate. These tend to diverse from the typical Owl outlined here in the extent of frill, the angle and length of beak and, in some, the presence of a crest.

The **African Owl** was imported into Europe in the 1850s. A smaller bird than the **English Owl**, it was also more finely developed. Its initial impact was to make fanciers attempt to breed the English Owl down in size, an unhappy but fortunately short-lived influence. The main difference between the present-day African and English Owls is one of size, and with that an understandable difference in head conformation, the English Owl being slightly longer in the face. The **Chinese Owl** is a popular variety in Germany. Its head is longer and more conventional. Frilling is the main feature, and this is more extensive than in the other Owls, with a large portion of the neck and breast feathers reversed. The underparts about the tops of the legs are also frilled and known as pantaloons. Germany has several other Owl varieties, among them the **Shield Owl**, a turbit-marked bird, and **Colored-tail Owl**. The latter, either plain-headed or crested, is bred in whites with colored tails and in colors with white tails.

English and African Owls are generally bred in solid colors, with blue and silver barred forms. Owls, particularly the African and Chinese, are delicate pigeons requiring great care on the part of the fancier to keep them healthy. As

Black-laced Satinette

Satinette Silverette

Turbiteen

Dun African Owl

113

with other short-beaked breeds, there are also rearing difficulties. Ordinary Tumblers make useful foster parents in this case.

DAMASCENE

The Damascene is an old Middle Eastern breed, once known as the Mahomet, noted for its particularly beautiful blue plumage. It is mentioned in pigeon literature from as far back as the latter half of the 17th century, but it has always been rare and today it is decidedly a minority interest. The Damascene is a short-beaked bird. It is thought to have been used at some point in the development of the English Owl. Black skin pigmentation and a fine sheen that gives the plumage an attractive damasked look, are major features. The Damascene is bred in icy blue with jet black wing bars. The eye cere is damson and fairly large.

Damascene

Black Checker English Owl

Yellow Chinese Owl

Red Shield German Owl

115

HYACINTH

The Hyacinth (classified by Lyell, 1887, as a French breed), is bred for its extraordinary color and markings. Some class it as a German toy, while others point out its similarity to the Starling (below). The Hyacinth is plain-headed and clean-legged. It is a shield-marked bird, the head, neck, body and tail being blue-black, with a darker bar at the end of the tail. The color is very rich and deep. Shields or saddles are creamy-ivory and marked with arrow-points of black within which there are triangles of gray. There is a white tip to each of the otherwise dark primaries. Hyacinths occur only rarely outside Germany.

LACENE

This British color pigeon is bred, as the name implies, for its laced wing plumage. Lacenes are solid color pigeons, coming in blues, blacks, reds, creams and yellows, with white wing coverts delicately laced. Each primary should be of the body color and "finch marked" (white tip). There are sulfur laces in which the wing ground is not white but a pale sulfur. The breed is of conventional pigeon size and line, generally plain-headed, but sometimes crested. It should have a red eye. Lacenes are a rare breed almost entirely restricted to Britain.

LAHORE

An exhibition pigeon of Persian origin, the Lahore was imported into Europe from India in the second half of the 19th century. Its markings are most distinctive. The Lahore is a white pigeon, colored on the crown, nape, upper back and wings. The demarcation between white and color is most striking about the head, where the color can either come half-way down the eye, or else skirts the upper half of the eye, leaving a thin line of white plumage. In some standards the latter is considered a fault. An early form has been described in which the beak was bicolored, the upper mandible dark and the lower light, but this feature has since been lost. The 19th-century Lahore was clean-legged, unlike the present-day grouse-legged version. The grousing probably derives from the **Sherajee**, an early subvariety of Lahore. Lahores are bred in blacks, blues, duns, lavenders, reds, silvers and yellows.

Hyacinth

Lacene

Black Lahore

Yellow Lahore

117

LARK

This breed consists of two varieties of German origin. The **Coburg Lark**, the product of either an Archangel-Scandaroon or Archangel-Roman Runt cross, is regarded as a table bird in Germany (see Section A). It has enjoyed a minority following in the US, but chiefly as an exhibition pigeon, being considered too small to compete with the large American utility breeds. The Coburg is plain-headed and clean-legged. It is broad in the shoulder, yet long enough in body for this to pass unnoticed, except of course when the bird is handled. Coburgs are bred in silver checks, in which the breast is bronze, and in barred and barless silvers, in which the breast is yellow. The tail is barred.

The **Nuremberg Lark** is a particularly attractive color pigeon, smaller than the Coburg, and of conventional type. Color and markings are the important features. The Nuremberg has a yellow head, neck and breast. The remainder of the bird, apart from wing markings and the terminal bar to the tail, is creamy white. There are two color varieties, silvers and checkers. In the silvers, the wings have two fine bars. In the checkers, the coverts are barred and checkered with black.

MONK

The Monk is a German toy pigeon, bred in plain-headed and crested, clean-legged and muffed varieties. Its name derives from the white or "bald" head, a monkish characteristic which is emphasized in the shell-crested variety, with its hooded appearance. In the less common clean-legged Monk, which is generally peak-crested, the colored plumage extends further up the back of the head than in the typical Monk. In some, the white head plumage extends a little way down the bib but, ideally, the line of demarcation should be about half an inch below the eye. Tail, primaries and muffs (the latter of moderate length) are white, while the remainder of the bird apart from the head is colored. Carriage is low. Monks are bred in barred and laced varieties and in blacks, blues, reds and yellows. In white bars, the lower edge of the bar is edged in black.

Coburg Lark

Nuremberg Lark

Muffed Monk

Clean-legged Monk

119

NUNS AND HELMETS

These two closely-related breeds are both noted for their head markings and feathering. Nuns and Helmets both have long histories through which their close resemblance to one another has given rise to a fair amount of confusion, particularly among the earlier commentators. The Nun is probably of German origin, although it is interesting to note that the French refer to it as a Dutch shell-crested pigeon. In some old authorities it is classed as a Tumbler (Section D). Fanciers who keep short-faced Tumblers have been known to use Nuns as foster birds. The **Spanish Nun** is a plain-headed highflying variety.

The **Nun** is basically white with colored head and bib, the head having a broad and full, but neatly-feathered, white crest. Primaries and tail are colored. In the last century a Nun with above six colored primaries was considered a good specimen. Nuns are active and easily managed birds. The chief problem is maintaining a good crest and good color demarcation. Fanciers have been known to indulge in plucking excercises to "improve" the line between colored and white feathering, but such ploys never escape close inspection. Nuns are bred chiefly in blacks, also in blues, silvers, reds and yellows.

Helmets are, like the Nun, basically white with a colored head. The wings are totally white, unlike those of the Nun, while the tail is colored, The cap of colored plumage should skirt the beet red cere for about two-thirds of its circumference. The crest should be of the shell type and should be moderately extensive. A well-domed, rather tumbler-like head is desired, with the beak short and stout. (Long faced birds also exist and are usually better breeders.) Helmets are chiefly exhibition birds but like Nuns are hardy and may be flown. They are sometimes bred in plain-headed forms, and occur in blues, reds, silvers and yellows.

Brown Helmet

Black Nun

Spanish Nun

Hamburg Helmet

121

PRIEST

The Priest is a German crested breed. There are two main varieties, the Double-crested and the Single-crested, of which the former is also a muffed pigeon. The **Double-crested Priest** is so called for its broad shell crest, which is terminated on either side by a small rose of reversed feathers, and for the reversed feathering above the beak. Muffing is fairly heavy. The colored plumage ends at a line from the base of the upper mandible, round the bottom edge of the eye, to the crest. White-barred blacks, blues, reds, silvers and yellows are popular and white laced blacks and blues are also bred. The **Single-crested Priest** also called Blassen lacks the crest above the beak and is clean-legged. It occurs in blacks, blues, reds and yellows. Barred blues and silvers and checkered blues are also bred.

PEAK CRESTS

Four Swiss varieties of peak-crested pigeons are covered by the general term Peak Crests. All are medium-sized birds of conventional outline, apart, that is, from being crested. Coloring and marking are the main points of interest.

The **Lucerne Peak Crests** are grouse-legged but clean-footed pigeons, sturdier birds than the other three varieties, with shorter and thicker beaks. Color variation is distinctive and wide in range. The **Copper Collar** is light blue with greeny-blue neck and copper-brown breast and comes in black-barred, checkered and barless forms. The **Gold Collar** is a mealy pigeon with dark yellow breast and a silver neck sheen. The brown form is marked in brownish-black. The **Lucerne Lark** is similar to the Gold Collar, but generally darker. The **Lucerne Elmers** are basically white with wing bars, neck and breast colored according to type, either yellow or brown. In the **Brown Elmer** the breast bears a brown crescent. Lucernes are also bred in solid blacks, blues, greys, mealies, reds, silvers, yellows and whites and in white-barred and laced forms.

Thurgau Peak Crests come in some of the same colours as the Lucernes. They are clean-legged, have a longer crest and are longer in the beak than the latter. Among the distinct Thurgau color varieties are the attractive shield-marked birds, in which the coverts are colored against a general ground of white. The **Thurgau Monk** is a monk-headed variety. In the **Thurgau White Tail** the entire bird is colored except for the tail and the undertail coverts, which are white.

Berne Peaks are bred in solid colors and in a wide range of color varieties, chief among them being the **Spot Tail**; the **Grizzle or Tiger Head**, in which the head is grizzled; the **Berne Lark**, which looks something like a much smaller version of the Coburg Lark (above); and the **White Tail**.

The fourth variety, the **Aargau Peak**, consists of two forms; the **Aargau White Tail** is peak-crested with a slender beak and body. It differs from all other Swiss breeds by having short thick muffs. The **Wiggertal Colored Tail** is peak-crested and clean-legged. The plumage is all white save for the feathers of the tail. Many colors exist in both varieties.

Double-crested Priest

White Lucerne Peak Crest

Berne Lark Peak Crest

Thurgau Shield Peak Crest

123

BREAST PIGEON

A German breed noted for its distinctive marking and feathering, the Breast Pigeon comes in plain-headed, crested and muffed forms. There are three main varieties. The **Old German Moorhead** is a sturdy black-and-white pigeon in which the head, bib and breast, and the tail are a solid black. It is bred in both plain-headed and crested forms, the crest being quite full and mane-like. The short legs appear to be even stumpier than they are, owing to the extensive muffs, in which the individual feathers are long and sweeping.

The **South German Breast** is an attractive, compact pigeon, perhaps the most appealing of the breed. It is colored about the head and bib in black, silver or yellow; the body should be a clean white, without any hint of lacing. This variety has a neater crest than that of the Old German Moorhead, though it too is quite full. The legs are clean. The stance is upright.

The **Saxon Breast** is a plain-headed, muffed variety in which the entire head, neck and breast is colored, black or yellow (the yellow form having a correspondingly pale beak). In all varieties the extent of the marking in the region of the breast and bib can vary considerably.

SHIELD

The Shield is a German Turbit-marked toy breed of which there are two main varieties. The **South German Shield** is a plain-headed and clean-legged variety, bred in a wide range of colors, including blacks, blues and reds, white-and black-barred blues, red-barred mealies and silvers. The simplicity of its line, a white bird of conventional type with strongly-colored coverts, is the key to its appeal.

Crested Shields are more elaborate and come in two main types: double- or single-crested, both being muffed. The body plumage, including the muffs, is white, the shields being colored. Colors are as for the South German Shield, with additional silver laces and silver blues. The double-crested form derives from a Bernburg Trumpeter cross (Section B). Plain-headed muffed forms also occur. Muffs are generally quite extensive.

South German Breast

Black Saxon Breast

Crested Muffed Shield

SPOT

The Spot, or Snip, is a German toy breed, named for the patch of color on the front of the head. Spots are both shell-crested and plain-headed and occur in muffed and clean-legged varieties. They resemble the Helmet (above), being white, head-marked birds with colored tails. They are, however, easily distinguished from Helmets. Head marking is far less extensive, generally taking the form of a symmetrical pear-shape or circle. The eyes are dark with narrow flesh-colored ceres. The beak is not only longer and more slender than in the Helmets, but it is also bi-colored, at least it is in well-developed specimens. The lower mandible is white, while the upper varies according to the spot color. Black and blue Spots have blackish upper mandibles. In reds and yellows the upper mandible is horn-colored. Muffs can be almost as extensive as those in the Swallows (Section B).

STARLING

This Thuringian German toy breed is noted for its spangle-marked black plumage. Starlings are clean-legged and come in shell-crested and plain-headed types. Marking is the chief feature, and is remarkable in its diversity. The **Marbled Starling** is a plain-headed black-and-white variety. The coverts are barred and laced white, and there are white tips to the primaries. There is also some white mottling on the breast. The Marbled probably derives from the **Barred or Starry-necked Starling**, a black bird with white wing bars and crescent breast marking.

Suabians or Silver-laced Starlings are lighter in color, having silver coverts and back, with the coverts laced. White-tailed varieties occur in all but the Barred Starling. There are also several varieties of **Monk Starlings** (shell-crested and white-headed). These come in the full range of markings described above. In simple White-barred blacks, the primaries generally lack the white tip. Starlings have also been bred in muffed forms, but the clean-legged variety is now preferred.

Monk Starling

Plain-headed Spot

Crested Spot

Marbled Starling

127

WHITE BIB

The White Bib, or Bavette, is a German head-marked and shell-crested toy pigeon. The White Bib has a monkish head, but in this case the white plumage extends down the face to about mid-breast. Feet should have neat white muffs and the tail is also white. The shell crest is of tidy cut. Seen from the side it can look rather like a pair of pricked-up ears. Among the wide range of varieties are blacks, blues, silvers and yellows; black-barred blues and checkered blues.

WHITE TAIL

This German toy variety is named for its white tail but the breed is also noted for the spot of white generally present on the forehead, above the base of the beak. There are a number of varieties. The **Muffed White Tail** occurs in both shell-crested and plain-headed forms. Muffing is extensive. The spot or snip is more of a blaze of white than in the other varieties. The Muffed White Tail is bred in white-barred blacks, blues, solid reds and yellows, in larks, and white and silver spangles, and in marbles and bronzes. The **Silesian White Tail** differs from the other varieties in lacking the spot mark. **South German White Tails** are spot-marked, muffed birds with white tails. The bird known in England during the last century as the Fire Pigeon or Fireback was probably an early form of the Dark Bronze South German White Tail, which is noted for its Archangel-like lustrous plumage (above).

SWIFT

A Middle Eastern breed, the Swift is noted for the flights and tail which are unusually long. There are two varieties. The **Egyptian Swift** is a short-faced pigeon, with a rather small, rounded head. The feet too are small and the legs short, giving the bird an ungainly appearance. Egyptian Swifts with wing-spans of over 32in have been recorded. Yet they make poor fliers. Feathering tends to be long throughout and somewhat loose. The variety is not a popular one but is kept on a small scale in the US. The **Syrian Swift** is a smaller, more practical bird, otherwise on the same lines as the Egyptian. It makes a good flier and is bred in attractive markings and colors, the laced indigos being highly prized.

Thuringian White Bib

South German White Tail

Egyptian Swift

D: PERFORMING PIGEONS AND RELATED VARIETIES

The Homer, Tumbler and assorted Highflier breeds treated in this section are all primarily performing pigeons. That is, they are bred for competitive flying. Over the years, however, fanciers have worked on these breeds to produce show varieties, the majority of which would, if put to it, prove poor performers indeed. Both schools are represented here.

HOMER

The name Homer is given to those strains of pigeon noted for their strong flight and ability to return "home" from considerable distances, and is also applied to related show varieties. The modern **Racing Homer**, as the performing Homers are chiefly known, is as much the product of selective breeding as any of the fancy pigeons. Yet it remains fairly close to the wild Rock Dove *Columba livia* in both appearance and hardiness. When Homers go astray their breeding is soon watered down in the pool of feral pigeon stock to swell the ranks of the common pigeon of city square and farmyard.

The domestic pigeon's value as a message bearer has been exploited from time immemorial. But the homing pigeon as we know it dates from the early 19th century. It has its origin in Belgium, at such centers as Antwerp and Liege, and in England. Apart from purely sporting interest, there was added commercial incentive to breed homing birds of speed, stamina and reliability in the practice begun by some Belgian financiers of using pigeons to carry the latest stock market reports from Paris and London. It is said that pigeon fanciers hired their birds out for this type of work and that competition thus grew between them. By 1850 there was also a well-organized pigeon post network between the larger Belgian cities.

Competitive racing began to evolve in Belgium during the early part of the century. In England, things started moving a little later with one of the earliest recorded races being from the town of Spalding in Lincolnshire to London, in 1872. At about the same time, with the importation of birds from Belgium, the sport was also being established in the US. Interest in pigeon racing is reputed to have been stimulated both in England and the US by the widely-reported use of pigeons in the Siege of Paris (1871) during the Franco-Prussian War, but presumably much had been happening prior to this in the way of selective breeding and racing.

Rock Dove *Columba livia*

Dovecot Pigeon *Columba affinis*

Dark-checkered Racing Homer

The chief breeds used in creating the **Racing Homer** are the now extinct Smerle and Horseman, and the early Cumulet (below), the Dragoon and the Carrier (Section A). Accounts of the Belgian Smerle, or Smerle of Liege, show that it was a strong if small flying bird capable of homing at speed from 500mi. Some authorities believe it to have derived from a Carrier-Owl or -Turbit cross, others that it was the product of a cross between the Cumulet, Owl and Turbit. It had a good full head, was deep-keeled and stout in the shoulder, and retained from the Owl and/or Turbit influence, a shortish beak and frilled breast. The Horseman was a variety of Carrier, between the English Carrier and Dragoon in size. Pouter (Section B) and Tumbler stock (below) were also important elements, the latter in the form of the Long-faced Beard, but there were many other ingredients in the melting pot. It was a matter of experimentation, with the birds' ability to home and to do so smartly, the guiding factors.

In the second half of the 19th century the various ingredients began to combine and there emerged a distinct Racing Homer. This brought together the best from Belgium, in the form of what is sometimes referred to as the **Flying Antwerp or Antwerp Carrier**, and the best from England. The English, working more slowly than the Belgians, had evolved a racing bird chiefly from Carrier stock, with Tumbler and Dragoon crosses the most significant. Belgian and Dutch fishermen-cum-pigeon fanciers are said to have played a significant role in the introduction of English birds to the continent. With these imports absorbed, the sport came to be dominated by a handful of individual strains, chiefly Belgian. One of the great names was that of the Belgian fancier N. Barker, whose stock of "Barkers" was sold to J. W. Logan of England in the late 1870s, a move which in time did much to strengthen the sport in England. Since then many famous strains have been established, with names such as Gits, Grooters, Pepermans, Van Rial, Vanderhaeghen and Osman, as well as Barker and Logan, being synonymous with the best in pigeon racing.

Today's pedigree Racing Homer might be described as twice the pigeon it was a hundred years ago. Birds capable of covering 1,000mi over two days, if not the happy possession of every fancier, are at least relatively common. Racing Homers of the European and American type are bred in any color, dark checkers being perhaps the commonest. Appearances can be deceptive, which being the case, it is safest to say that a good bird is one with a sound flying record. A full head, broad chest and straight keel, combined with a generally healthy appearance, are obvious guidelines, but the most unlikely bird can turn out to be the winner among many a finer-looking specimen.

Racing Homers are also bred in the Middle East. Of these the **Syrian Dewlap** is a particularly fine example, noted for its strength and size. The name refers to the thickened and slightly pendulous, or dewlapped throat. This is the most distinctive physical feature, although the size of the dewlap varies widely from specimen to specimen. The breed is rare outside the Middle East and there is, unfortunately, very little known about it. Of the several varieties the commonest are blue checkers and bars. These often have white flight feathers and are marked with a white blaze on the front of the head and

Red-checkered Racing Homer

Black Racing Homer

Blue-barred Racing Homer

Syrian Dewlap

133

additional white patches high on the neck. Dewlaps are alert in appearance and have an impressively powerful, driving flight.

The **Lebanon** is a form of Dewlap, some specimens of which have been imported into the US. It is a bird of great potential, as a racer, show or table bird. The dewlap is less pronounced than in the Dewlaps proper and the white head markings are absent. Among the major color varieties are reds, yellows; reds and yellows with white tail bars and flight ends; white-barred blacks with white tails, the wings and tail being laced and the breast having a white crescent; white-barred blues and light blues; and laced light blues.

During the course of the European and American Racing Homer's development a number of by-roads were taken by fanciers more interested in exhibiting than racing their pigeons, and several "show homer" varieties were gradually evolved. Among the earliest of these were the British **Show Antwerps**, a direct offshoot of Antwerp Carrier stock. There are now two recognized varieties: the Short- and the Long-faced Antwerp. A medium-faced variety, the existence of which tended to threaten the cultivation of a truly distinctively faced pigeon, fell from favor in the 1920s. The Show Antwerp enjoyed a great vogue in the late 19th and early 20th centuries. Most of its properties are those of head. In the **Short-faced Antwerp** the front of the typically dark beak should be short, blunt and massive. The head has to be big. All the curves should be convex, wattle and cere filling out the shape. Barb and Runt crosses were used in the breed's development, although Barb crosses were considered something of a risk as they tended to produce a projecting cere, thus spoiling the curve of the head. For the **Long-faced Antwerp** the properties should be the same, but with the face longer, more as for the Show Homer (below) but not quite so full. The Show Antwerps are sturdy birds of general Homer type. The eye is a bright red, a good point of identification as it helps differentiate between the Antwerps and most other show Homer varieties.

Closely related to the Show Antwerp but possibly more impressive is the **German Show or Beauty Homer**, a bird of striking looks, derived from Germany's Racing Homer through outcrosses on the Show Antwerp and Show Homer (below). A highly popular fancy in its native country, it is now established farther afield, particularly in the US. Elegance of head structure and carriage are the hallmarks of this bird. The long, slim neck is carried almost at right-angles to the horizontally held body and tail. Head and beak form an unbroken, tight curve. The bright red eye of the Show Antwerp is retained and is distinguished in this case by its tendency to protrude. The ceres are a fine gray.

In the **Giant Homer** we have a comparatively recent US creation, produced from heavy squabbing birds through the Show Homer (below), during the 1920s. It enjoys a wide following as a show pigeon and is, in addition, a popular table bird. The name is quite appropriate: the Giant is a broad-shouldered, short-bodied pigeon capable of weighing well over 24oz. It is also a prolific type and this of course makes it ideal for commercial purposes.

The **Exhibition Homer** is a variety of the sturdier Show Homer (below). It

Lebanon

Short-faced Antwerp

Long-faced Antwerp

Red German Show Homer or Beauty Homer

135

is largely restricted to Britain where it was first developed, in the early part of this century. The Exhibition is thought to have resulted from a series of crosses between the Show Homer and other Homer types. A broad-bodied bird with a distinctive upright posture, it has a firm plumage and carries its wings close. These features give it a strong, compact appearance. The face is long and the beak straight and stout. A dark cere contrasts with the pearl eye.

An impressive Roman-nosed British exhibition pigeon, the **Show Homer**, evolved more or less in the same period as did the Show Antwerp. Head and beak provide the main points. Ideally the two should form a strong continuous curve, of which the wattle should be an integral part. There is an unusually great length of face from the pearl-colored eye to the base of the typically thick beak. The Show Homer is stocky and short-winged. Feathering is generally tight. Weight can reach 28oz.

The **American Show Homer** is a more conventional bird. It tends to be short-necked and is rather upright in station. The head and beak present a fuller curve than is found in performing pigeons, but a less pronounced one than in for example, the German Show Homer (above). The cere tends to be absolutely minimal in this variety.

Show Homer

Giant Homer

Exhibition Homer

Show Homer

137

TUMBLER

The name Tumbler originally applied to a breed of pigeons of Asian origin noted for their habit of tumbling or somersaulting in flight. It is now used for both performing and show varieties, the latter being by far the larger group. As the drift away from flying to showing gathered pace during the second half of the 19th century, fanciers interested in the Tumbler's aerial performance began to evolve specialized flying types. These have been classed separately as Rollers, Tipplers and Flights (all dealt with below). True Tumblers bred for performance are said to be of the Common Tumbler type. But this designation is sometimes confusing as, in some regions, the term Tumbler is also applied to Tippler pigeons and, as will be seen, the modern Tippler is not bred for its tumbling or tippling flight but for its ability to keep airborne over a long period. The phenomenon of tumbling is something of a mystery. There have been numerous attempts to account for it, ranging from the one prevalent in Victorian times that it was related to epilepsy, to the more recent belief that it is caused by an inherited defect of the bird's inner ear. Whatever the answer, pigeons of good tumbling ability are something of a rarity nowadays.

English show Tumblers are bred in two major categories: the Short- and the Long-faced, each coming in a wide range of color varieties, the latter proving something of a misnomer when compared with European Long-faced Tumblers (below).

The **English Short-faced Tumbler** enjoyed great popularity during the latter half of the 19th century when it was noted as much for its color qualities as for the line of its head. The perfect head, short and round with an abruptly rising, even overhanging, frontal (referred to as the "stop" or "bulge"), was often pursued by artificial means. This activity is described in the following way by one writer of the period: "In regard to the heads, however, it is necessary to state that at one time very few birds were shown whose heads had not been tampered with, an implement of wood being pressed into the bottom of the forehead daily, from the time the bird was a few days old, till the skull was 'set'.... The process is one of very great cruelty, the skull being literally crushed into shape, with immediately fatal results in scores of cases."

The palish, horn-colored beak is short and fine and points straight out, any tendency to look downfaced being undesirable. Wattling is small and must be fine. The eye is prominent, with the pupil black and iris white, and is surrounded by a neat cere. It is set well down, thus emphasizing the full nature of the head. The Short-faced Tumblers were developed to carry their wings below the tail. This feature is not always observed, and is positively disliked in the US.

The **Almond** has for a long time been the dominant color variety. In this the yellow body is spangled with black, primaries and main tail feathers containing distinct yellow, black and white marking. A splashed form of Almond exists in which the black spangling is more intense and the yellow is largely absent from primaries and tail. The body is also splashed with white. **Kites** are black with bronze on the tail and flights, the black having considerable sheen. **Agates** are white-splashed reds. **Baldheads** are white

English Short-faced Tumbler

English Long-faced Tumbler

in the head, flights, undersides and tail. The remainder of the bird is colored. White head feathering should extend clearly below the eye, to a depth of just under $\frac{1}{4}$in. Colors are black, blue, cream, dun, mealy, red, silver and yellow.

The **Beard** is a bird resembling the Baldhead, except for the head marking. The head is colored and bearded white at the upper bib. The beard extends back to form a point under and coextensive with the eye. **Mottles** are solid colored with white mottling on the wings and in a V-shape on the back, at the base of the neck. White birds are bred with black mottling. Other colors are black, red and yellow. **Rosewings** lack the mottling on the back but otherwise resemble Mottles.

The **English Long-faced Tumbler** is bred in two main types, muffed and clean-legged. It is a short, thick-bodied bird in which wings and tail are also short. Unlike the Short-faced, it carries its wings smartly above the tail. The eye is the same as in the Short-faced, but is situated at the center of the bird's distinctly round head. The head should be broad across the front. Any tendency towards an oval head with even a slight hollow to the face should be strongly avoided. Markings and colors are similar to those in the Short-faced Tumbler, differences occurring between the muffed and the clean-legged varieties. **Muffed Long-faced Tumblers** are bred in self-colors and in badge, beard, baldheads and saddles also in almonds, rosewing, whitesides and mottles. The muffs are well developed giving the bird its squat appearance. **Clean-legged Long-faced Tumblers** are bred in self-colors, checkers, bars, grizzles, baldheads and beards also in straight mottles, rosewing and whiteside and mottles of both.

The contrast between the European Long-faced Tumblers and their English namesakes could hardly be more stark. Birds such as the Danish and German Long-faced Tumblers are truly long in the face. Both breeds contain several interesting varieties. The **Danish Long-face** is a lengthy, sleek pigeon, long in body, wing and tail, with the legs, head and beak also long. It is moderately down-faced. A number of color varieties are bred, including self-coloreds. The *stripper* marked bird comes in silvers, whites and yellows with black flecking. The *brander* is a deep rich red bird with metallic green hackles and black flights and tail. Other forms are tiger; white-flight; white-tailed white flight, and helmet.

German Long-faced Tumblers include the **Elster or German Magpie**, a magpie-marked pigeon, long in body, leg, head and beak; the **White-flighted White-tailed Long-face**, a rangy bird in which the beak is unusually lengthy and slender; and the **Brunswick Beard**, which is similar to the German Magpie. Germany also has a division of **Medium-faced Tumblers**. This includes the **Hanover Red-eye**, **Hanover White-eye**, the **Pomeranian**, the **Bremen**, the **Stargard Shaker**, the **Ringbeater**, the **Cologne** (in clean-legged and muffed forms), and the **Gumbinnen**.

German Magpie Tumbler

Danish Long-faced Tumbler

Clean-legged Long-faced
Baldhead Tumbler

Brunswick Beard

141

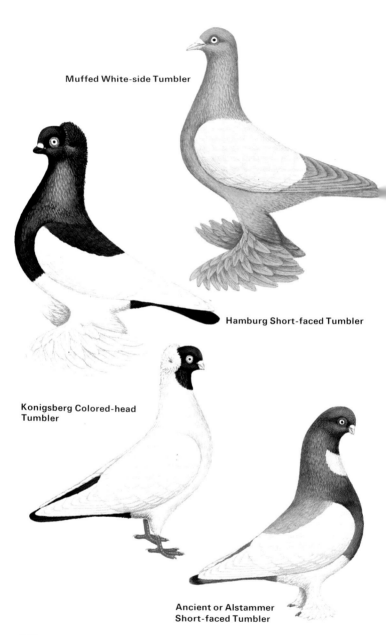

Muffed White-side Tumbler

Hamburg Short-faced Tumbler

Konigsberg Colored-head Tumbler

Ancient or Alstammer Short-faced Tumbler

142

The German Short-faced Tumblers are a large and important group. One of the major varieties is the **Hamburg Short-faced Tumbler**. This is bred in helmets; white-tails; white-flighted white-tails; tigers; magpies; tail-marks; nuns and white-selfs. The **Ancient or Altstammer Short-faced Tumbler** is a pronouncedly short-faced pigeon with a good round and broad head and a short down-faced beak. It is a stocky bird of neat appearance and is bred in pieds, which at their best have a white bib marking, and in tigers as well as in other colors. The legs are groused. Another short-faced variety is the **Konigsberg Colored-head**, a Moorhead Tumbler. It is a shell-crested, muffed variety and is distinctly marked, being white with the head and upper bib and the tail colored (black, blue, red, white or yellow). The **Posen Colored-head** is a clean-legged version of the Konigsberg. Other German short-faced Tumblers are the **Elbing White-head**, the **Reinaugen**, the **Stettiner** and the **Märken Magpie**.

Germany is an important center for the groups of Tumblers classed together as **Hungarian Pigeons** and consisting of medium- and short-faced pigeons of Austrian, Czechoslovakian and Hungarian origin. In this group, one of the most popular varieties is the highflying and show bird, the **Vienna Medium-faced Tumbler**. It is a small and slender pigeon, relatively long in the leg and neck and with an alert appearance. When showing it should stand with the first or hind toe clear of the ground. There is an unusual small bulge at the back skull. The eye is full and round, dark at the pupil with the iris white or pearl. The beak is dark in color and points straight out. Several color varieties are bred, the most common being the White-storked or Hell-storked bird in which a white plumage is offset by dark flights and tail end. Sometimes there is a light print through the body and the neck can be grizzled grayish, undesirable features in birds bred for showing. Other color varieties include the violet and

Vienna White Stork Tumbler

green; blue self-colored and Strasser-marked. The **Vienna Short-faced Tumbler** is in contrast a fairly stocky pigeon. It has a neat somewhat Barb-like head (Section A). The eye is full and is surrounded by a full red cere. Vienna Short-faces are bred in selfs, in white-flights and in magpies or gansels. In the latter the head, nape and upper breast are white, as are the wings legs and underparts, the remainder, including the tail, being colored black, blue, mealy, red or yellow.

The **Komorner Tumbler** is another of the Hungarian group. It is a shell-crested variety, somewhat stocky, with a small rounded head. The beak is of medium length, the face moderately short. Komorners are bred both as show birds and performing highfliers. The crest is a full one, punctuated on either side of the head by a small rose of reversed feathers. Color varieties include magpies, which are white headed and bearded, with the wings and underparts white also. The remainder of the bird including the crest is colored. Komorners are also bred in self-colors including the barred forms. Other Tumblers in the Hungarian Pigeon group are the **Szegediner, Prague, Budapest, Egri, Koros** and **Bacska Tumblers**.

As has already been suggested, the Tumbler breed is named for what amounts to a somewhat freakish trait. This trait is no longer found in a great many of the breed's varieties. But in one it is present in an extreme form. This is the **Lotan**, an Indian ground-tumbler, of which Charles Darwin wrote: "These birds when gently shaken and placed on the ground immediately begin tumbling head over heels, and they continue thus to tumble until taken up and soothed,—the ceremony being generally to blow in their faces, as in recovering a person from a state of hypnotism or mesmerism. It is asserted that they will continue to roll over till they die." The Lotan is a medium-sized peak-crested bird with feathered feet, reported as being most commonly bred in whites. Lotans are fancied on a small scale in parts of the US.

Similar in the extremity of its behavior to the Lotan, but perhaps more appealing, is the **Parlor or House Tumbler**, a diminutive pigeon of otherwise common Tumbler type. It is unusual in its habit of tumbling at very low heights (never much more than 3ft from the ground, often within a few inches). The variety was cultivated in the 19th century in Scotland, where it was known as the House Tumbler, and in the US. There are three distinct standards of performance: single, double and rolling, backward somersaults. The double should consist of an ascending and descending tumble. The roll consists of a sustained, rapid sequence. During the performance the bird should be as close to the ground as possible.

An example of the way in which Tumbler varieties can hover, as it were, between being bred for performance or for show may be seen in the case of the **West of England Tumbler**. This is a competent performer, generally giving single somersaults but sometimes throwing back in a sequence of three or more and capable of sustained highflying. However, it is also an unusually attractive bird, being bred in a wide range of colors and markings. It is thus gaining ground in the show rooms. The West is noted for its contrasts of color against clean, white feathering. Colors include blacks, blues, grizzles, reds, red checks, mealies and yellows.

Yellow Vienna Short-faced Tumbler

Kormorner Tumbler

145

ROLLER

This is a type, rather than a variety of Tumbler, selected and cultivated for its spinning or rolling when in flight. Rollers might be called the thoroughbred performers of the Tumbler family. They do not, however, always breed to standard and individuals can be relegated to Tumbler status, even after a moderate career as a Roller. The standard of flight is the deciding factor. Rollers should be capable of somersaulting backwards at great speed and over a considerable distance. What this amounts to in fact is an average of about a dozen spins over a fall of some 12ft. Birds capable of rolling for dives of more than 20ft are not uncommon. A roll is actually achieved by the bird's trying while in mid-air to touch its tail with the back of its head and revolving in the attempt, rather as a dog does when it chases its tail. The revolutions should be concentric and balanced. Rollers will also perform conventional tumbles. They are usually flown in large kits, the habit of rolling seeming to be contagious: once one or two birds in a kit start, the others will generally join in, providing a truly startling spectacle.

As performance is the major factor, Rollers tend to be bred in any of a wide range of colors. There are two main types. The famous **Birmingham Roller** is a neat little pigeon with a well domed head. It has an alert appearance and the eye has that bright look common to performing birds. Birminghams are bred in white-heads, white-flights and -tails, bell-necks, beards, badges and saddles, in other words the full range of Tumbler markings.

The **Oriental Roller** may have played a part in the early development of the Birmingham, but this part is likely to have been no more than a very small one. Orientals are Asian birds, somewhat loose-feathered, and, as they trail their wings down below the tail, are nowhere near as spritely in appearance as the Birmingham. In performance they can do well, provided they fly with their own kind, and provided their flight feathers are in good shape, which is not always an easy thing to ensure in pigeons that trail rather than carry their wings. Orientals are noted for their strong colors and are particularly attractive in blacks, reds and yellows. West of England Tumblers (above) are sometimes incorrectly lumped together and called Rollers. Individual Wests might, however, prove to have good rolling ability. Among the Hungarian Pigeons (see Tumblers, above), there is a shell-crested highflier, the Koros Tumbler, which is said to have considerable aerial talent.

Almond Birmingham Roller

Oriental Roller

Baldhead Birmingham Roller

Hungarian Roller

TIPPLER

A flying variety of the Tumbler family, Tipplers, which are also bred for showing, are of conventional Tumbler line. They carry rather than trail their wings and are bred in many colors and patterns. Competitive Tippler flying is based upon endurance. The birds are trained to stay on the wing and within sight of the loft (except for the first hour's flying) for as long as possible. A signal flag is used to direct them and lure birds to call them down. When in training the birds are pushed to do times of about 15 hours and more. Winning times of between 18 and 20 hours are on record. The Cumulet (below) is thought to have played some part in the development of the **Flying Tippler.**

Show Tipplers are bred in four varieties; Dark Mottles, Selfs, Light Mottles and Chucks. The Dark Mottle is brown with white markings and the Self is a solid brown color with a black bar across the end of the primaries, secondaries and tail feathers. The Light Mottle is white with brown markings. The Chuck is pure white with the exception of the chuck or bib, tail and primary flights, which are brown. The brown is a deep chocolate color derived from a cross with the Brander.

Self-bronzed Tippler

Light-mottle Show Tippler

149

CUMULET

Cumulet is an English name for a French breed of highflier known in France as *pigeon monte-au-ciel* (the pigeon that climbs to the sky). The term "cumulet" clearly echoes the French name in its suggestion of "cumulus," the round masses of white cotton-wool cloud common to summer skies. A good high-flying pigeon can climb above 3,500ft, the height around which cumulus usually rides. So it would be possible for Cumulets to disappear into such cloud masses.

As performing pigeons Cumulets are, however, regarded as average, largely because, though graceful and attractive, they lack the versatility of other highflying breeds. Apart from a tendency to clap their wings and glide, they are closest to the Tipplers (above) in their performance. Indeed the Cumulet is said to have been instrumental in the development of Flying Tipplers. It was also a basic ingredient in the creation of the modern Racing Homer (above). A show variety has been developed, primarily in Britain and the US.

A medium-sized pigeon, the Cumulet was originally bred in blacks and reds, with the flights and tail white. Today it is a white pigeon, though white adults with red bibs or red or yellow ticks or flecks at the neck are also known. Young birds too sometimes show red neck marking. Ideally the Cumulet should have a fine rather than a domed Tumbler-type head, and the white beak should stand out well. Wattle and cere are delicate and also white in color. The eye should be pearl, with a small black pupil. (See also Highflier, below.)

FLIGHT

This US breed is in two quite distinct white-flighted varieties. The **Domestic Flight** is a highflying pigeon traditionally flown from city rooftop lofts, particularly in New York City. Domestic Flight kits are trained rather in the same way as the early Modenas (Section C) to lure other kits away from their lofts, a ransom being set for the return of captured birds. The sport was once extremely popular but has declined a great deal with the rapid urban growth of the last 40 years. The Domestic Flight is believed to have originated from a Magpie-German Medium-faced Tumbler cross. It is of medium size and comes in plain-headed and crested forms. The front skull rises quite steeply from the barely-wattled, flesh-colored beak. The eye should be white with a delicate cere. Domestic Flights are bred in mottles, in blacks, reds, yellows and duns and in blue, mealy and silver barred forms.

The **Show Flight** is an exhibition variety. It has retained much more of the Magpie influence than has the Domestic, possibly through the additional medium of the Martham. The Show Flight falls somewhat between two stools, lacking the neatness of its highflying cousin on the one hand and the refinement of the Magpie on the other. It shoud be upright in posture, long in leg and neck, with the lines of head and beak tapering down evenly. The beak should be stout and should measure $1-1\frac{1}{4}$in. Colors are as for the Domestic Flight.

Flying Cumulet

Show Cumulet

Domestic Flight

Show Flight

HIGHFLIER

Highflier varieties are noted, like the Cumulet (above), for their high flying. The major continental Highfliers form a somewhat ill-defined group. The **Russian** and **Polish Highfliers** are not identical breeds, but they are certainly closely related, and both are similar to the Cumulet and to the **Stralsund Highflier** of Germany, though this bird has a flatter crown. All four are longish birds with fine beaks and fairly full faces. The **Belgian Highflier** is a more thickset bird than those so far mentioned; it is closely related to the **Dutch Highflier**, which however is a bird of finer cut. Of the continental Highfliers, the most impressive is the **Danzig**, a bird of very different lines from the others. It is shell-crested and has an unusually full tail which suggests likely Fantail influence (Section B). However its tail (14–20 feathers) does not appear to interfere with its flying ability; it is towed along, stiff and arched during flight. The Danzig resembles the Cumulet and the central European Highfliers in having a moderately long face, slender beak and slim line. Danzigs are bred for the show room as well as for performance and come in blacks, reds, yellows, whites and in tigers and mottles.

Russian Highflier

Polish Highflier

White-saddled Belgian Highflier

Danzig Highflier

153

BIBLIOGRAPHY

The following works represent some of the classics of pigeon literature, most of which are now collectors' pieces.

ALLDRIDGE, R. W.   Carrier Pigeons. 1871

BIGNOLD, G.   The Pigeon Fanciers Assistant. London. 1848

BLANCHON, H. L. A.   Manuel pratique de l'éleveur de pigeons. Paris. 1899

BRENT, B. P.   The Pigeon Book. Three Editions. 1860, 1865 and 1871

BROAD and FIRTH   Carriers and Barbs. London. 1898

BRUNO, H. W. B.   The Longfaced Tumbler. London. 1904

BURGESS, J. L.   The Belgian Homing Pigeon. London. 1881 and 1882

COLE, L. J. and F. J. KELLEY   Studies on inheritance in pigeons. 1919

DARWIN, Charles   The Variation of animals and plants under domestication. London. 1868

DIETZ, E. J. W.   A to Z on Pigeons. The Item Publishing Co. 1929

DIXON, E. S.   The Dovecote and the Aviary. London. 1851

DODGE, H. E.   The Racing Homer. London. 1921

EATON, J. M.   A treatise on the art of breeding and managing tame domestic and fancy pigeons. London. 1852

FLETCHER, W. R.   Dragoons. London. 1908

FULTON, R.   The illustrated book of pigeons with standards for judging. London. 1876. Also the Book of Pigeons revised by Rev. W. F. Lumley. 1895

GOODALL, A. A.   The archangel pigeon. London. The Feathered World 1924

HARRIS, E. D.   The structure, flights and habits of the different varieties of the domestic pigeon. Boston. USA 1878

HAZARD, F. A.   Profitable pigeon breeding. USA

HEPWORTH, A. F.   The Tippler pigeon up to date. London. 1893

HOLMES, W. E.   The Modena pigeon. Watmough Ltd. 1921

HOUSE, C. A.   Magpies. Watmough Ltd. 1912

——   In-breeding. Watmough Ltd. 1935

——   Pigeons and all about them. Watmough Ltd. 1920

LONG, J. C.   The Feather's practical pigeon book. Washington. 1903

LUCAS, J.   The Pleasures of a Pigeon Fancier. London. 1886

LUMLEY, Rev. W. F.   Pigeons, their origins and variations. London. 1895

LYELL, J. C.   Fancy Pigeons. London 1881 and later editions

MACHIN, F.   The Oriental Frill Pigeon. Birmingham. 1919

MOEBES, Werner, K. G.   Prolific writer of pigeon literature including Bibliographie der tauben (Germany)

MOORES, J.   Columbarium: or, the Pigeon House. London. 1735

LEVI, Wendel M.   The Pigeon. The Encyclopedia of Pigeon Breeds. (Sumter, S. C., USA) (and many others)

NAETHER, C. A. Prof.   The Book of the Pigeon. Chicago 1940

RICE, E. C.   National Standard Squab Book. Cambridge. Mass. Many Eds.

ROGER, J.   Pigeons, how to rear, breed and keep. London. 1880

SCATLIFF, H. P.   The Modern Turbit. London. 1906

SEATON, H.   Oriental Frills. 1912

SIMPSON, Wm. Jnr.   Standard of Excellence of the National Columbarian Society. USA. 1879

SPRUIJT, C. A. M.   Several works between 1922 and 1938

TEGETMEIER, W. B.   Pigeons. London. 1868, and the Homing or Carrier Pigeon 1871

TWOMBLY, C. E.   The Pigeon Standard. Medford. Mass. USA

URE, G.   Our Fancy Pigeons. Dundee. 1886

INDEX

Page numbers in italics refer to
illustrations or their captions.